WARSHIPS IN FOCUS
THE NAVAL PHOTOGRAPHY OF MICHAEL LENNON

PLAYING WITH THE BIG BOYS!

During Staff College Sea Days on 26th May 1983 HMS HUNTER, London division RNR tender, passes the Type 22 frigate HMS BATTLEAXE at speed during manoeuvres in the Solent.

First published in the United Kingdom in 2016 by NavyBooks, Unit 6B, Heathlands, Liskeard, Cornwall, PL14 4DH

Printed by FINIDR, Czech Republic

INTRODUCTION

My earliest memories of the Royal Navy would have been in the early 1950's. Family holidays to the Isle of Wight, via the car ferry from Old Portsmouth to Fishbourne, took us past HMS Vernon and HMS Dolphin with the large number of minesweepers, torpedo boats and submarines tied up alongside making an unforgettable impression on a young school boy. As we neared the island I recall passing the old aircraft carrier HMS FORMIDABLE. She had been laid up at anchor in the Solent for several years and was only towed away to shipbreakers in May 1953, just before Queen Elizabeth's Coronation Review which took place the following month. I guess it would not have looked good to have her spoiling the impeccable review lines!

My father managed to secure the family places on a dockyard tug to witness the review though, unfortunately, it would be another 10 years before I owned a camera - so many photographic opportunities were missed during my early years.

Summer holidays to Devon always included a day trip to Plymouth with a river cruise up the Tamar to 'View the Warships' and, as a schoolboy I was a keen collector of warship photographs - my sources were many - Wright and Logan; Tom Molland; Real Photographs and the Pavia Brothers from Malta.

My father had worked in Portsmouth dockyard since the late 1940's and in 1961 was posted to Gibraltar on a three year tour. Our family sailed on the troopship DEVONSHIRE from Southampton early in February 1961 arriving a few days later. Whilst approaching the Rock a squadron of American Gearing class destroyers passed very close to our ship.

In September of 1961 I started an electrical apprenticeship in H.M. Dockyard Gibraltar. The naval base was extremely busy in the early 1960's and Coaling Island was home to many laid up Ton class minesweepers. These resident ships required ongoing refits, as did those from the 9th Minesweeping Squadron arriving from and returning to their base in the Persian Gulf. Refits of frigates, destroyers and assistance to visiting warships kept the dockyard busy.

In 1963 my father gave me my first camera - a Photina twin-lens reflex format 6x6. At this time the whole of the harbour was controlled by the military so with no access to either the dockyard or commercial harbour the only chance for ship photography was from my 13ft dingy and of course very much dependent on the weather. My father again came to my rescue. He knew the Base Intelligence Officer and a casual conversation with this gentleman resulted in my being given a permit to photograph ships entering and leaving harbour - the start of a hobby that has lasted for more than 50 years.

There was much to photograph. The dockyard was always full and during the annual *Dawn Breeze* exercises there could be as many as 70 warships and attendant oilers and support vessels berthed - sometimes three or four deep; all available space taken up by the visiting international fleets. The Rock was so busy that on occasion extra tugs would be sent from the UK or Malta to help out.

In 1964 we returned to the UK. I continued with my apprenticeship with weekends at Old Portsmouth photographing from the Round Tower - but I still returned to Gibraltar for holidays over the following years. In 1966 I completed my indentures as a Gyro Compass technician and worked on many RN ships, as well as two minehunters converted for Argentina in HM Dockyard, Portsmouth and the former submarine TOTEM, sold to Israel and lost in the Mediterranean on its delivery voyage.

In 1968 I was back in Gibraltar and took up a position with the Ton class minesweeper refit group where there was always at least one in refit. In 1971 the last two Tons in reserve at Gibraltar were re-activated and, after maintenance, were sold for service with the Irish Naval Service. On completion of the refits sea trials were undertaken and trips to the Algarve or Tangier were often included during these work ups.

In 1973 I returned to Portsmouth and continued with the Portsmouth CMS refit group. Good opportunities for my ship photography continued and trips to most naval bases were undertaken. In 1974 I took up employment with Vosper Thornycroft at their Woolston Shipyard although the day that I started there the whole workforce walked out on strike. I don't think that I was the cause !!

By 1975 I had made the decision to become a full time photographer. Over the following years I attended many naval reviews, commissionings and sea trials as well as receiving invitations to go to sea on exercises and naval press days. In 1980 I joined the RNR Solent Division at HMS Wessex, serving on several Ton class ships and taking part in exercises such as *Rockhaul*, *Springtrain* and *Damsel Fair* with trips to Gibraltar and the Mediterranean as far east as Sicily.

Since my first camera, the Photina, I pretty much stayed with the 6x6 format throughout although the original was just fitted with a standard 80mm lens. I progressed through Yashicamat which was also restricted to its 80mm optics. The way forward was with Mamiya 220 / 330 which gave the option of several different focal length lenses. I dabbled with the larger format Mamiya press but always came back to my favourite 6x6. Right up to middle of 2010 I was still shooting black and white and colour transparencies. Never used colour negative film. Always felt comfortable with monochrome but, since 2010 I succumbed to the modern day digital as Black and White was becoming too expensive.

ACKNOWLEDGEMENTS

In 2015 Maritime Books suggested that perhaps I would have enough material to put together a book, illustrated with my photographs taken over more than 50 years. Here is the finished article showing an even spread of pictures between the years 1963-2013. The photographs up to 2010 are all from my monochrome negatives with the remaining three years being black and white scans from my digital colour images. I have tried to use views that have not previously been used to illustrate other publications but, over such a long number of years, some may have slipped in by mistake. My apologies if this is the case.

My association with Maritime Books goes back to about 1978 when I was asked to supply photographs for inclusion in their new book, *British Warships & Auxiliaries*. After 38 years I am still a contributor to this handy little reference book.

Over the years I have had a great deal of assistance from so many individuals. Too many to name individually. Public Relations Officers within MoD(N), Shipping Masters from Gibraltar, Portsmouth, Portland, Devonport, Pembroke Dock, the Clyde, Rosyth and Chatham when the auxiliary vessels were operated by the Royal Maritime Auxiliary Service.

I am indebted to my long suffering wife Frankie for putting up with my 'hobby' for so long. My children Michael, Jason and Sarah for assistance with computer and related IT subjects. David Whiteside for helping to scan my monochrome negatives and Mikey Jirku for assistance with the digital colour images.

I would also like to mention my late father in law Mr Douglas Brett RMAS, the master of auxiliary vessels ARLINGHAM at Gibraltar and DOWNHAM and OILMAN as well as the salvage vessel PINTAIL at Plymouth. Many days were spent on the latter down at Falmouth when maintaining the moorings in and around the river Fal. I would also thank Mr Dave Moody, the coxswain of the pilot vessels L03 and L42 at Portsmouth, and the late Mr Peter Sleet, piermaster at Kings Stairs, Portsmouth who never refused a request for a trip out on the pilot boat; always sanctioned by those up top, of course.

A final thanks to Mike Critchley for sewing the seed, Steve Bush for pushing this project forward and to Ian Whitehouse for agreeing to publish this book - perhaps, if it proves popular I may be persuaded to dig deeper into my archives for a further volume!

Michael Lennon
Waterlooville, 2016

Built by Camper and Nicholson as HMS AMERTON. She was one of the numerically large Ton class of coastal minesweepers constructed in the 1950's. Seen here at Gibraltar in 1963, she was renamed for the Glasgow division of the Royal Naval Reserve (RNR) as HMS CLYDE, here returning from a weekend visit to Tangier during exercise Rockhaul, the annual visit of the RNR's 10th Minesweeping Squadron. In this picture CLYDE, having the squadron commanding officers broad black band painted on the funnel, leads the rest of the ships through the Bay of Gibraltar into harbour.

HMS MURRAY, one of 12 Type 14, single screw anti-submarine frigates known as the Blackwood or Captain class, all constructed in the late 1950's in various UK shipyards. She is seen entering Gibraltar in September 1963. She was built on the Clyde at the Alexander Stephen Govan yard completing in 1956. On this visit to Gibraltar she was attached to the 2nd Frigate Squadron. Her main armament comprised two triple barrelled Limbo Mk10 ASW mortars, sited aft. A further three Type 14's were built for the Indian Navy in British shipyards.

HM Tug VAGRANT built at the Scott Bowling yard in 1943 as the EMPIRE TITANIA. One of a large class of WW2 tugs built for the British government, she served at Naples, then Chatham before finally transferring to Gibraltar in 1959. She was operated by the Port Auxiliary Service, the forerunner of the RMAS. In her role at Gibraltar she was used for general harbour and local towage. She was replaced in 1967 by the Dog class tug SEALYHAM and, in 1968, was sold to Sicilian interests and renamed ZANCLE under the Italian flag. She was broken up at La Spezia in 1987. In the picture to her right is the Ton class minesweeper OULSTON which was put into reserve on completion of building. She never commissioned into the RN being sold to the Irish Navy in 1971 as LÉ GRAINNE.

5

Heading out from Gibraltar in October 1963 for another summer in the South Atlantic and Antarctic is HMS PROTECTOR. She was built at Yarrows, Glasgow as a net layer and completed in 1936. She was refitted as an Ice Patrol Ship at Devonport in 1954 and fitted with a rudimentary hangar and flight deck for two Westland Whirlwind helicopters. She made her first Antarctic patrol in the winter of 1955/56, serving the Falkland Islands and the British Antarctic Survey bases. She was to return to the Antarctic a further 13 times before decommissioning in 1968. She was sold for breaking up in 1970.

Seen entering Gibraltar dockyard on 26th November 1963 by the south entrance, HMS DIAMOND makes an impressive picture in the late evening sun. She was one of a class of eight destroyers of the Daring class, all constructed between 1952-4. DIAMOND was built at John Brown's yard on the Clyde, being launched in June 1950 and commissioned on 21 February 1952. At the time the photograph was taken she was a member of the 23rd Escort Squadron. In 1970 she became an alongside training ship moored off Gosport and remained so until towed away for breaking up on the Medway in 1981.

The Reserve Fleet headquarters ship HMS SHEFFIELD is moored alongside the former Inshore Minesweeper Flotilla Base Ship HMS MULL OF GALLOWAY in Portsmouth harbour in 1964. SHEFFIELD was completed in 1937 at Vickers-Armstrong Yard on the Tyne as one of the Southampton class cruisers. She was known throughout the fleet, as were her successors, as the *Shiny Sheff*, as her adopted city donated stainless steel deck fittings during her construction. She saw extensive action during WW2 and had an active post-war career, including a starring role in the film '*The Battle of the River Plate*' in which she portrayed the cruiser HMS AJAX. In September 1964 she was placed on the disposal list and broken up at Faslane in 1967.

The Royal Fleet Auxiliary RFA TIDEPOOL at anchor off Gibraltar in February 1964. Classified as a Fast Fleet Replenishment Oiler she was built, with her sister ship TIDESPRING, at the Hebburn yard of Hawthorn Leslie Shipbuilders and completed in 1963. During the 1970s the ship took part in both the Cod Wars and the Beira Patrol, the blockading of oil shipments to Rhodesia through Mozambique. She was sold to Chile in 1982 but, whilst on delivery, was temporarily requisitioned for service during the Falklands War. At cessation of hostilities she was finally handed over to the Chilean government and renamed ALMIRANTE JORGE MONTT.

HMS ALBION heads home to Portsmouth in April 1964 from Gibraltar with her paying off pennant flying after service in the Far East. She was one of the three Centaur class aircraft carriers ordered during WW2. A fourth, HMS HERMES, was of a similar design. ALBION was built on the Tyne and completed in 1954. She was converted at Portsmouth Dockyard to a Commando Carrier during 1961-2 before sailing for the Far East where she saw action during the Borneo conflict. At the time it was normal for ships to fly a paying off pennant prior to decommissioning for a long refit, unlike today when ships pay off into reserve or for disposal. ALBION was broken up at Faslane in 1973.

HMS OWEN was laid down in 1944 at the Hall Russell yard at Aberdeen. She was to have been one of the numerically large Loch class anti-submarine frigates and named LOCH MUICK, a name chosen by King George VI as the loch runs near Balmoral. She was, however, launched in 1945 as HMS THURSO BAY an anti-aircraft frigate but was completed at Chatham Dockyard as a survey ship, the fourth in the Cook class. Photographed leaving Gibraltar on 10th May 1964 flying her paying off pennant, after oceanographic work off Malta, she finally decommissioned at Devonport in 1965. She was placed in reserve and ultimately broken up at Blyth in 1970.

Designed for use during the Pacific War, HMS ASTUTE was laid down in 1944 at Vickers Barrow yard and completed in 1945. She was one of a large number of 'A' class submarines ordered during the 1940's but was completed too late to see war service - of the 46 submarines ordered only 18 were launched. As the Cold War heated up, the role of the submarine changed from targetting surface ships to sinking submarines. From the 1950s the 'A' class were modernised and streamlined to improve underwater speed and reduce noise. HMS ASTUTE was loaned to the Royal Canadian Navy on two occasions before joining the 2nd Submarine Squadron at Devonport in 1963. Pictured on a visit to Gibraltar in June 1964, she was sold for scrap in 1970.

Britain's first nuclear powered submarine HMS DREADNOUGHT is seen entering Portsmouth Naval Base on 22nd May 1965. She was built at Barrow-in-Furness by Vickers Armstrong, completing in 1963. She was powered by an American nuclear reactor manufactured by Westinghouse Electric Company and spent several months experimenting with different types of propellers operating out of Gibraltar in 1964. In March 1971 she became the first RN submarine to surface at the North Pole and two years later was a part of the RNs first annual group deployment. In 1977 she deployed to the South Atlantic, with the frigates ALACRITY and PHOEBE to deter possible Argentine aggression towards the Falkland Islands. She decommissioned in 1980 and remains (2016) laid up at Rosyth dockyard.

An early morning view taken on 28th of June 1965 showing HMS TIGER departing from Portsmouth flying the flag of Admiral Michael Pollock, Second in Command, Home Fleet. To have been named BELLEROPHON, one of the Minotaur Class cruisers, she was built by John Brown's shipyard on the Clyde. She was laid up after being launched in 1945 in an incomplete condition. Work did not restart until 1954 and she was finally commissioned in 1959. The class comprised three ships, her two sisters being LION and BLAKE. In 1966, she hosted talks between Prime Ministers Harold Wilson (UK) and Ian Smith of Rhodesia. She paid off into reserve in 1966. Between 1968-72 she was converted at Devonport to a helicopter cruiser. Her after 6-inch and midship 3-inch turrets were removed and replaced with a flight deck and hangar to operate Wessex helicopters. In 1986 was towed from Portsmouth to Spain for breaking-up.

HMS GRAFTON, a Type 14 anti-submarine frigate passes the hot walls, Portsmouth, outbound for trials in the English Channel in June 1965. Built on the Isle of Wight at Cowes by J. Samuel White and completed in 1957. She served for six years with the 2nd Frigate Squadron at Portland after which the ship started a refit at Portsmouth Dockyard. She was then attached to the 20th Frigate Squadron based at Londonderry, Northern Ireland, before paying off in 1969. She was broken up at Inverkeithing, Scotland from December 1971.

Leaving Portsmouth in June 1965 after being laid up there since 1961 is the 'O' class frigate HMS ORWELL under tow bound for the ship breaking yard of J. Cashmere at Newport. Built by John I. Thornycroft at Woolston and completed in 1942. One of a class of eight destroyers constructed during WW2, all survived to the end of hostilities. She saw action at the Battle of the Barents Sea, and was involved in convoy escort duties during the Battle of North Cape. Post war she was part of the Portsmouth Local Flotilla and used for torpedo training. With a desperate shortage of fast anti-submarine ships she underwent a limited conversion at Rosyth dockyard in 1952, emerging a year later as a Type 16 frigate. She was sold for scrap to John Cashmore Ltd and arrived at Newport for breaking on 28 June 1965.

The Ton class coastal minesweeper HMS LEVERTON at speed off Rosia Bay, Gibraltar, heading for the naval base in the summer of 1965. Built by Harland and Wolff at Belfast and commissioned in 1955, she was originally constructed with Mirlees main engines. She was converted at Plymouth Dockyard and fitted with high speed Napier Deltic's in the late 1950's. Seen here on an operational visit to the Rock, she was, at the time, part of the 7th Minesweeping Squadron based at Malta. In 1969 the 7th MSS left Malta and arrived at Gibraltar either to pay off into reserve at the Coaling Island minesweeper base or for onward return to the United Kingdom. LEVERTON was sold for breaking up by Pounds at Portsmouth and demolished in 1971. She was named after a village in Lincolnshire.

The Admiralty Cable Ship (ACS) BULLFINCH at anchor off the south mole Gibraltar on a beautiful August evening in 1965. She was built in 1940 by Swan Hunter and Wigham Richardson at their Low Walker yard on the River Tyne. She was one of four sister ships built for the Admiralty by this company. In the late 1940's two were transferred for service with Cable and Wireless and the last one of the four to be in service, ST. MARGARETS, was eventually transferred to the RMAS and survived into the 1980's.

HMS LEVIATHAN seen laid up in Portsmouth harbour in 1965. She was built by Swan Hunter at their Tyneside yard and launched in 1945 as one of the Majestic class of light aircraft-carriers but too late for war service and was never completed. She spent her life moored in Portsmouth harbour. She was slowly stripped of parts to maintain her sisters and, following a boiler room fire in KAREL DOORMAN (ex-VENERABLE), her turbines and boilers were stripped out and installed when that ship was refitted following a sale to Argentina. LEVIATHAN was also used as an accommodation ship for refitting carriers at Portsmouth. She was broken up in Scotland in 1968.

The Boom Defence Vessel MOORLAND, one of a class of net layers built between 1938-46. She was operated by the Port Auxiliary Service along with her sister ship MOORHILL for the maintenance of the buoys and moorings in and around Gibraltar. This shows her with a danger/keep clear flag flying attending one of the harbour moorings in the summer of 1965; not much activity visible on deck so most likely at the crews lunch or siesta time! MOORLAND was disposed of in the 1960's. She was the last permanently based vessel of this type at Gibraltar. In the future moorings would be serviced by craft sent from Malta or the UK.

The 'T' class submarine HMS TALENT photographed from the Round Tower inbound to HMS DOLPHIN in 1965. Built at Barrow by Vickers Armstrong, she was completed in 1945. Originally to have been named TASMAN her name was changed when an earlier TALENT of the same type, built in 1943, was transferred, also in that year, to the Dutch Navy. Several of the class were lost during the war. On 15 December 1954 she was swept out of drydock at Chatham Dockyard when the dock gate lifted, an accident that claimed four lives. She was reconstructed between 1954 and 1956, when she was streamlined and modernised. She paid off in 1966 and was broken up at Troon in 1970.

The Ton class minesweeper HMS THAMES pictured entering Portsmouth in 1965 to berth at the minesweeping base HMS VERNON. She was built as HMS BUTTINGTON by Fleetlands Shipyard at Gosport and completed in 1954. She was transferred to the London division of the RNR in 1961 as the tender to that division but based at Southampton rather than in the centre of the capital. The picture shows her with the old Type 974 radar. She had Napier Deltic engines fitted during a refit in the early 1960's. She paid off for disposal in 1967 and was broken up at Newhaven in 1970.

HMS BLACKPOOL was one of six Type 12 frigates built for the Royal Navy. Specialist anti-submarine frigates, they were armed with two triple-barrelled Mk10 Limbo AS mortars aft and more sophisticated sensors than their smaller and utility Type 14 contemporaries. Her AS sensors and armament were complemented by a twin 4.5-in gun and improved air and surface search radar. BLACKPOOL is pictured leaving Portsmouth on 8th September 1966 at the start of a five-year loan period to the Royal New Zealand Navy. She was built at Belfast by Harland and Wolff and completed in 1958. On her return to the RN she was decommissioned and converted at Portsmouth dockyard to a trials and target ship. Towed to Scotland in March 1976 she was eventually broken up on the Forth in 1978.

Flying her paying off pennant HMS AGINCOURT arrives home at Portsmouth for the last time on 10th September 1966 to enter the reserve fleet. Built on the Tyne at the Hawthorn Leslie shipyard and completed in 1947, she was one of a large number of Battle class destroyers constructed in various shipyards in the late 1940's. In 1959 she, along with three sister ships, started a refit to convert them to Fleet Radar Pickets. At this time the Type 965 AKE-2 radar, also known as the "double bedstead", on top of the newly constructed foremast was installed. A Seacat missile launcher was also added. During her last commission she was part of the 23rd Escort Squadron operating in the Mediterranean. After eight years in reserve she was broken up in Sunderland in 1974.

RFA OLNA a fast fleet tanker, is seen approaching the harbour entrance at Portsmouth, in ballast. The Ol-class tankers were tasked with providing fuel, food, fresh water, ammunition and other supplies to RN vessels, while underway, around the world. In this picture, taken in 1966, she was on her first visit to the naval base. Constructed at the Tyneside yard of Hawthorn Leslie, and launched in 1965 and completed in early 1966, she was one of three sister ships built for the Royal Fleet Auxiliary. A similar ship was ordered by the Imperial Iranian Navy but was not delivered until several years after the overthrow of the Shah in 1979. OLNA saw service during the Falklands War. She was finally paid off in 2000 after 34 years of service, going to an Indian breakers yard in 2001.

Pictured off Gibraltar in August 1967 during Exercise Rockhaul HMS DUFTON had replaced HMS BUTTINGTON as tender to London division RNR. At the time she was photographed she had not been renamed to bring her into line with other RNR ships and their local divisions. Built at Goole and commissioned in 1955 she saw service in the Mediterranean and then the Far East. Like most Ton's on operations during the Malaysian confrontation with Indonesia she was fitted with a second 40mm Bofors aft of the funnel in place of the original 20mm Oerlikon. Decommissioned in 1969 she was broken up at Sittingbourne in 1977.

The Ton class minesweeper HMS CHAWTON departing Gibraltar in 1967 after a long refit, bound for Bahrain via the Cape of Good Hope. This was to be her last commission east of Suez. She was built at Fleetlands, Gosport, and completed in 1958. She saw service at Malta and Singapore before moving to the Gulf of Oman in 1965 to join the 9th Minesweeping Squadron. In 1969 she returned to Gibraltar to refit and was then placed in reserve at Coaling Island before commissioning in the Fishery Protection Squadron in 1971 as a replacement for the damaged BELTON. In 1975 she paid off for disposal, finally being broken up at Middlesborough in 1977. Chawton is a village in the North of Hampshire, near Alton, famous as the home of the authoress Jane Austen.

Seen moored off Gosport in 1967 is the Weapon class destroyer HMS CROSSBOW. Built by John I. Thornycroft at Woolston and completed in 1948. She was one of four sister ships, though there were plans for a much larger class, most of which were cancelled at the end of WW2. All four of the class were converted to Fleet Radar Picket's, CROSSBOW being refitted at Chatham Dockyard between 1957-9. In 1963 she paid off into the reserve fleet, before becoming a harbour training ship attached to HMS SULTAN in 1966, replacing the earlier battle class destroyer SOLEBAY in that role. Subsequently CROSSBOW was replaced by the Daring class destroyer DIAMOND in 1970 and put on the disposal list in that year. She was sold to Thomas Ward at Briton Ferry for breaking up in 1972.

The Type 15 anti-submarine frigate, HMS WAKEFUL pictured departing Portsmouth on a sunny July morning in 1967. At that time she was attached to the 2nd Frigate Squadron. She was built at Fairfield's Shipbuilding yard at Govan, and completed in 1944 as one of eight "W" class destroyers. She saw war service in the Atlantic, Indian and Pacific Oceans. She was converted at Greenock by Scott's Shipbuilding Company between 1951-3 to a Type 15 frigate. All superstructure to deck level was removed and replaced with a lower structure extending aft to the quarterdeck. The principal anti-submarine armament was a pair of Mark 10 Limbo A/S mortars. In 1970 she was placed on the disposal list and in 1971 was broken up at Inverkeithing by Thomas Ward.

29

Constructed during WW2 as one of eight 'U' class destroyers, UNDAUNTED was built at Birkenhead by Cammell Laird. Completed in 1944, she took part in the Normandy Landings and was in operations against the German battleship TIRPITZ off Norway. She also saw service in the Mediterranean operating out of Malta and was present at Yokohama for the surrender of the Japanese forces on VJ day. UNDAUNTED paid off into reserve at Devonport in 1946. In 1953 she started conversion at Samuel White's yard at Cowes on the Isle of Wight to a Type 15 anti-submarine frigate completing in 1954. Fitted with a flight deck in 1959 she carried a Wasp helicopter, seen here in this photograph taken in July 1967. In 1973 she paid off into reserve and was expended as a target in 1978 in the Atlantic to the west of Gibraltar.

One of the 'Leaf' class of medium freighting tankers, RFA BRAMBLELEAF was photographed entering Gibraltar through the north entrance in the winter of 1968. Built by Furness Shipbuilding Co. at Stockton-on-Tees for London Greeks as the M/V LONDON LOYALTY she was completed in 1954 and chartered by the RFA in 1959. She was renamed BRAMBLELEAF and operated for the MoD until 1972 when the charter ended and was returned to her original owners who named her M/V MAYFAIR LOYALTY. In 1974 she was broken up at La Spezia, Italy.

One of 26 Leander class frigates built for the RN, HMS CLEOPATRA is seen arriving in Gibraltar in 1968. At this time she was attached to the 8th Frigate Squadron. Built at Devonport dockyard she was commissioned in 1966. In 1973 she operated off Iceland during the Cod War. From 1973-75 she underwent an extensive modernisation at Devonport - her 4.5-inch gun turret was removed and four MM38 Exocet missile launchers fitted on the forecastle. A quadruple Sea Cat missile launcher was fitted forward and an enlarged hangar enabled a further two launchers to be fitted on the hangar roof. The removal of the AS mortar provide a larger flightdeck for a Lynx helicopter. Decommissioned in 1992 she was sold for scrap the following year.

The Whitby class frigate HMS EASTBOURNE seen at Gibraltar in 1968. Laid down in 1954 at the Vickers Armstrong Yard on the Tyne, she was however completed at their Barrow yard in 1958. At the time of this visit to the Rock she was part of the 5th Frigate Squadron. In 1972 she replaced the Type 15 frigate RAPID as the training ship for artificers from HMS CALEDONIA. In 1976 she was damaged in a collision with the Icelandic Gunboat BALDUR during the Cod Wars. A hull inspection during the subsequent repair period found that the ship was no longer fit for sea, but her machinery was sound - her propellors were removed to enable her to be run at full power while remaining alongside in the training role. She finally decommissioned in 1984 and was sold for scrap in 1985.

Another Gibraltar visitor was the Rothesay Type 12M anti-submarine frigate LOWESTOFT. The Type 12M was a development of the Type 12 but with a modi-fied after deckhouse, enlarged to carry the Sea Cat anti-aircraft missile launcher and its associated GWS-20 director and handling rooms as it became available. From the 1960s the class was taken in hand for modernisation. The foremost set of AS mortars was removed and the well plated over to provide a small flight-deck for a Wasp helicopter and the aft superstructure was replaced by a small hangar with the Sea Cat mounted on the roof, as seen here. Built at Glasgow by Alex Stephens and completed in 1961 she was one of nine ships in this class. Used as a target she was sunk by a torpedo fired from HMS CONQUEROR in 1986.

The destroyer HMS CAPRICE on the D.G. range at Gibraltar during post refit trials in 1969. One of eight 'Ca' class war built destroyers, she was constructed at Yarrows shipyard on the Clyde and completed in 1944. Originally to have been named SWALLOW she was renamed CAPRICE before her launch. In 1966 she was modernised by the addition of the Sea Cat system on an enlarged after deck house, together with two Squid AS mortars. In 1968 she took part in the Beira Patrol as part of the oil blockade against Rhodesia. She ended her career as an Engineer Officer training ship, day running from her base at Devonport. She paid off in 1973 and was broken up at Queenborough on the Isle of Sheppey in 1969. Her sister CAVALIER is preserved as a museum ship at Chatham.

The County class destroyer HMS LONDON arriving at Gibraltar in 1969 with Admiral Sir Varyl Begg, Gibraltar's new Governor and Commander in Chief embarked. Built by Swan Hunters at Wallsend she commissioned in 1963. One of a class of eight built in the early 1960's, the later four in the class were converted to carry Exocet missiles in place of 'B' turret. She took part in the Silver Jubilee Fleet Review in 1977. The ship was the last RN vessel capable of firing the Mk 1 Sea Slug missile and, on 10 December 1981, the last RN ship to fire a four-gun broadside. She paid off at the end of 1981 and was sold to Pakistan the following year. She served as PNS BABUR until decommissioning in 1993 and being sold for scrap in 1995.

The Landing Ship Logistic SIR GERAINT awaits her pilot off Gibraltar in 1969. Built by Alexander Stephen she was completed in 1967. At the time of the photograph the "Sirs" were operated for the MoD by the British India Steam Navigation Company in their corporate livery of white hull with a blue band and buff funnel. In 1970 they were transferred to RFA management and adopted the more familiar all-over grey appearance. RFA SIR GERAINT operated out of Marchwood Military Port in Southampton. On 28 March 1970 she sailed with RFA EMPIRE GULL from Tobruk for the final withdrawal of British Forces from Libya. She saw service in the South Atlantic during the Falklands War, was decommissioned in 2003 and broken up in 2005 at Gadani Beach, Pakistan.

RFA SEA SALVOR arrives at Gibraltar towing the Dog class tug AIREDALE from Malta in 1969. Built at Goole, she was completed in 1944 as one of the King Salvor class salvage ships. In August 1949 together with RFA DISPENSER and the salvage vessel RETRIEVE she was involved in the raising of HMS BRECONSHIRE from Marsaxlokk Harbour, Malta where she had sunk in March 1942. In 1956 she was involved in the raising of wrecks from the canal following the Suez crisis. Based at Malta she was, in her later years, support ship to the 7th Minesweeping Squadron. Having paid off for disposal in 1971 she was towed to Devonport by the tug RFA BUSTLER and was sold for scrap in 1973, arriving at Grays, Essex on 18th January of that year.

Liverpool's RNR tender HMS MERSEY during 'cheer ship routine' in the straits of Gibraltar in the summer of 1969 whilst on Exercise Rockhaul. Completed in 1958 as HMS POLLINGTON, she was built by Camper and Nicholson at Gosport. A member of the 10th, formerly 101st Minesweeping Squadron of the RNR, she served continuously with Liverpool RNR from 1959 through to 1975 when she was placed in reserve. She was recommissioned into the Fishery Protection Squadron in 1978 and finally paid off for disposal in 1985. She was broken up at Cairnryan in 1987.

Off Europa Point, Gibraltar, on Exercise Rockhaul in 1969, HMS MONTROSE is seen here as leader of the 10th MSS. Built at Whites shipyard, Southampton she was first commissioned in 1955 as HMS DALSWINTON. In 1961 she joined the Tay division of the 101st MSS squadron, being based at Dundee. In 1962 the 101st became the 10th and she continued to serve as tender to Tay division until paying off in 1972. She was sold to Pounds at Portsmouth for breaking up in 1973.

RFA BROWN RANGER, one of a class of war built small replenishment tankers, pictured alongside the fuelling jetty at Gibraltar in January 1970. A total of six of this type were built. GRAY RANGER was a war loss. Built by Harland and Wolff and completed in 1941 she saw convoy service in the Mediterranean and also served in the Pacific during WW2. Between 1950-3 she was in operations during the Korean conflict. Decommissioned in 1974 she was towed from Portsmouth in May 1975 for breaking up in Spain.

Built by Thornycroft at their Woolston yard HMS DUNCAN was commissioned in October 1958 as one of the 12 Type 14 anti-submarine frigates completed for the Royal Navy in the mid 1950's. She served as Leader Fishery Protection Squadron from 1958 to 1965. Following a refit at Rosyth she became an ASW training ship at Londonderry. She is pictured here off the north mole on the D.G. range after a refit at Gibraltar Dockyard in 1970. She would return to the UK to join the 2nd Frigate Squadron. In 1971 she replaced SAINTES as the harbour tender to HMS CALEDONIA at Rosyth. She was placed on the disposal list in 1978 and broken up on the Medway in 1985.

The Whitby class Type 12 anti-submarine frigate HMS SCARBOROUGH anchored off Gibraltar airport in 1970 on guard ship duties. Built on the Tyne by Vickers Armstrong she was first commissioned in 1957. She was the only one of the Whitby class to retain her original funnel throughout her RN service. At the time this photograph was taken she was part of the Dartmouth Training Squadron and was a regular visitor to the Rock. She decommissioned in 1972 and was laid up at Devonport. She was towed to the Tyne in March 1973 for a survey by Swan Hunter Shipbuilders and returned the same month. In 1974 a proposed sale to Pakistan was cancelled and in 1977 the ship left the Tyne, where she had been laid up for several months, was towed to Blyth Shipbreaking & Repairers for breaking up.

One of four Salisbury or Cathedral class Type 61 aircraft direction frigates HMS LLANDAFF is pictured leaving Gibraltar in 1970 on return to the UK to pay off. Built by Hawthorn Leslie on the Tyne, she was commissioned in 1958. They were powered, not by steam, but by eight Admiralty Standard Range ASR1 diesels. This limited their top speed but gave them increased endurance to help in their envisaged role of air ocean surveillance ship and air control ship to escort slow task forces, such as amphibious task forces. The diesel exhausts were housed within the mast structure thereby negating the need for a conventional funnel. LLANDAFF was transferred to the Bangladeshi Navy in 1976 and renamed UMAR FAROOQ.

The Royal Fleet Auxiliary replenishment tanker ORANGELEAF entering Gibraltar harbour in 1970 with the Dog class tug AIREDALE secured on her port side. Also alongside is the GENERAL ELLIOT, one of the Gibraltar Port customs launches. She was built by Furness Shipbuilding and was completed in 1955 as the M/V SOUTHERN SATELLITE for the South Georgia Company under Christian Salveson Management. Bare-boat chartered to the Admiralty in 1959, she was renamed ORANGELEAF and converted to RFA specification by Barclay Curle shipbuilders at their Glasgow yard in the same year. She saw service during the Second Cod War off Iceland in June 1973. She was returned to her owners at Singapore in 1978 and broken up in South Korea in the same year.

HMS VERULAM seen passing the detached mole at Gibraltar on a sunny afternoon in the autumn of 1970. Built at Govan by Fairfields, she was one of eight "V" class destroyers constructed during WW2. The leader of the flotilla HMS HARDY was lost during WW2. Five of the class were converted to fast anti-submarine frigates under the Type 15 programme, but unlike the earlier ships seen in this book the V class were equipped with Squid AS mortars in lieu of Limbo due to insufficient funds existing to fit all ships with Limbo. The remaining two unconverted V class were sold to the Royal Canadian Navy in 1944. At the time of her visit to Gibraltar VERULAM was part of the 2nd Frigate Squadron. She paid off in 1970 and was sold for scrap to John Cashmore Ltd, Newport.

HMS PENELOPE was built by Vickers Armstrong on the Tyne and completed in 1963 as one of the Leander class general purpose frigates. Ordered initially as the fifth of the Type 61 aircraft direction frigates she was to have been named COVENTRY. In 1966 she started a refit that would see her serve as an important trials ship over the next decade. In the picture, showing her at Gibraltar in 1968, her Seacat missile system and 40mm Bofors, along with the Limbo triple barrel depth charge launcher and some of her radar fit, had been removed. Her twin 4.5-inch guns and associated direction equipment were in a preserved state and would shortly also be removed. She was to take part in noise trials with propellers removed and all machinery shut down and sole power for steering supplied from boxed generator sets on the flight deck. She was towed by her sister ship HMS SCYLLA at speeds of up to 23 knots on the end of a 6000ft manila cable which stretched a further 25% when under load. This exercise took place to the east of Gibraltar in 1970.

The Daring class destroyer HMS DEFENDER pictured at Gibraltar in the summer of 1970. On this visit she acted as depot ship to the 10th MSS on their annual visit for Exercise Rockhaul. Constructed by Alexander Stephen and Son at their Govan Shipyard and completed in December 1952 she was involved in the Korean War and conflicts in Malaya, Cyprus, Suez and Aden. DEFENDER also attended the Coronation Fleet Review in 1953. On her return from Gibraltar she paid off and was listed for disposal. She spent her last days in the Firth of Forth on target trials before being sold for breaking up in 1972.

Senior ship of the 10th MSS, HMS THAMES follows HMS DEFENDER through the north entrance at Gibraltar in 1970 ahead of the rest of the squadron at the start of exercise Rockhaul. Built as HMS WOOLASTON by Herd and Mackenzie at Buckie, she was first commissioned in 1958. Her first deployment was to Malta, before going on to the Far East and seeing action during patrols off North Borneo. During one incident a booby-trapped sampan exploded alongside killing one trainee officer. She later served with the 8th MSS at Hong Kong before taking passage to Gibraltar and arriving in April 1968 where she paid off for a long refit. She returned to the UK after her refit where she commissioned for London division RNR as HMS THAMES. HMS WOOLASTON had the pennant number M 1194 and indeed left Gibraltar with this number on her hull. Somehow she managed to appear back in Gibraltar in 1970 wearing the pennant number M 1117 of the scrapped HMS BUTTINGTON. She eventually paid off in 1975 and went to the breakers in 1980.

RFA SIR GALAHAD, a 'Sir' class Landing Ship Logistic, she is photographed arriving at Gibraltar in 1971. All LSL's operated out of Marchwood Military Port on Southampton water. SIR GALAHAD took part in the Falklands War, sailing from Devonport on 6 April 1982 with 350 Royal Marines embarked. On 24 May she was hit by a 1000lb bomb, during an air attack, which failed to detonate. Then, on 8th June whilst preparing to off load Welsh Guards off Fitzroy, she was again bombed and set alight resulting in 48 fatalities. On 21 June, being deemed too badly damaged, she was towed out into deep waters and sunk by HMS ONYX. She is now designated a war grave.

Heading into Gibraltar dockyard in 1971 is the Fleet Replenishment Ship RFA RESURGENT. One of a pair of former passenger/cargo ships, they were purchased by the Admiralty in 1954 from the China Navigation Company. RESURGENT, the former M/V CHANG CHOW and her sister RETAINER ex M/V CHUNG KING were both built by Scotts of Greenock in 1951 and 1950 respectively. The Admiralty purchased both ships and after employing them for a while on charter work, they were converted in 1957, by Vickers Armstrong (Shipbuilders) Ltd at Palmers Hebburn Yard on the Tyne, into Armament Stores Issuing Ships, although they also carried a proportion of Victualling Stores too. RESURGENT served until 1979 and was broken up in Spain in 1981.

The submarine depot ship HMS FORTH flying her paying off pennant, heads home to the UK from Gibraltar in June 1971 having left Singapore earlier that year. Built on the river Clyde at John Browns Shipyard she commissioned in 1939. During WW2 she was based at Holy Loch on the Clyde and Trincomalee, Ceylon. Post war she was based at Malta, where she became a familiar sight at Msida Creek. Between 1962-66 she was modernised to support nuclear-powered submarines after which she served in Singapore supporting the 7th Submarine Squadron. She returned to the UK and in 1972 was renamed HMS DEFIANCE for service at Devonport (*see page 73*).

Seen here in her role as Gibraltar's permanent guard ship HMS ARLINGHAM comes alongside her berth at north mole in 1971. The crew look very relaxed at the end of one of their patrol's out into the bay where they were constantly making their presence known to the regular Spanish naval vessels that would anchor off the rock. Clearly visible at the bow is the ships dog, Chokka, which arrived at Gibraltar on HMS SHAVINGTON when the 7th MSS transferred from Malta in 1969. ARLINGHAM, built by Camper and Nicholson, was one of a numerically large number of Inshore Minesweepers of the Ham class, all built in the 1950's. She was one of several to be converted to Torpedo Recovery Vessels and was then based at Gibraltar and operated, with a civilian crew, by the PAS. In 1969 she was transferred back to the Royal Navy and operated by HMS ROOKE, in her role as guard ship. ARLINGHAM was named after a village in Gloucestershire. She was sold locally in 1978.

The nuclear-powered submarine HMS CHURCHILL pictured in the summer of 1971 at speed heading off into the Mediterranean from Gibraltar. Built at Vickers yard in Barrow in Furness and completed in 1970 she was the first of three of her class. CHURCHILL was chosen to trial the first full-size submarine pump jet propulsion. Trials of a high-speed unit were followed by further trials with a low-speed unit, and these were successful enough for the revolutionary propulsion system to be fitted to subsequent submarine designs. She was present at the Queen's Silver Jubilee Fleet Review in June 1977. She was decommissioned in 1991 and remains laid up at Rosyth dockyard.

The Air Store Support Ship RFA RELIANT was built at Sunderland and completed in 1954 as the M/V SOMERSBY for the Ropner Shipping Company. She was purchased by the Admiralty and commissioned into the Royal Fleet Auxiliary under her original name. In 1958 she was converted at Smith's Dock, North Shields, to a Stores Issuing Ship and was renamed RELIANT. She was extensively equipped for replenishment at sea with 6 replenishment points, carried 2 x 42 ft naval storing tenders and had a limited VERTREP capability. Photographed leaving Gibraltar in 1971, she was broken up at Inverkeithing in 1977.

Leader of the eight 'U' class war built destroyers HMS GRENVILLE is seen at Gibraltar in the early 70's. Built by Swan Hunter on the Tyne and commissioned in 1943, she was named after Sir Richard Grenville, a famous sailor from the reign of Queen Elizabeth I. She saw action during the Anzio landings and was also present at Normandy for the D-day landings. She also saw service east of Suez towards the end of hostilities against the Japanese. In 1953 she started conversion to a Type 15 anti-submarine frigate completing in 1954. GRENVILLE was laid up at Gibraltar from 1960-64. In June 1964 she was towed to Portsmouth and started a refit, reappearing, with a very modern looking foremast, as a trials ship for the Admiralty Surface Weapons Establishment. Over the next few years GRENVILLE was used to trial various new radar sets whilst attached to the 2nd Frigate Squadron. Finally paying off in 1974 and going for scrap in 1983.

The former Colossus class aircraft carrier HMS TRIUMPH steams into Gibraltar flying her paying off pennant with two Wasp helicopters on her deck on her return to the UK following service in the Far East. She was built on the Tyne by Hawthorn Leslie and completed in 1946. She saw service during the Korean conflict after which she was selected to replace HMS DEVONSHIRE as a cadet training ship. She carried two terms each of 100 RN and Commonwealth cadets on three cruises each year to the West Indies, Scandinavia and around the UK, and to the Mediterranean. In 1956 she began a conversion at Portsmouth to a Heavy Repair Ship. On completion she was based in Singapore. On her return to the UK she was laid up at Chatham Naval base until 1981 when towed to Spain for breaking up.

An 'A' class submarine HMS ANDREW heads out of Gibraltar in 1972. Built by Vickers Armstrong at Barrow, she was completed in 1948. These diesel-electric sub-marines were designed for use in the Pacific War. Only two were completed before the end of hostilities, but following modernisation in the 1950s, they continued to serve in the Royal Navy into the 1970s. HMS ANDREW was the last in the class to have a 4-inch deck gun fitted - it was mounted in 1964 for service during the Indonesia-Malaysia confrontation to counter blockade running junks. HMS ANDREW carried out the last gun action surface on 3 December 1974. A signal was relayed to the Royal Navy, Australian, Canadian and US navies reading "*The reek of cordite has passed from the Royal Navy's Submarine Service. Last gun action surface conducted at 031330Z. Time to first round, 36 seconds. May the art of submarine gunnery rest in peace but never be forgotten.*" The gun was AURIGA's fitted on ANDREW after refit. She was sold to be broken up for scrap on 5 May 1977, the work being conducted by Davis and Cann Ltd at Plymouth.

One of two Fearless class assault ships, HMS INTREPID arrives at Gibraltar in the summer of 1972. She was built by John Brown's on the Clyde, and completed in 1967. Designed as Landing Platform Docks, they were able to transport and land troops by sea using Landing Craft Utility, which operated via a well deck or helicopters. Both ships were part of the task force sent to recapture the Falklands Islands in 1982. At the time INTREPID was in the process of being decommissioned for sale but she was rapidly returned to service. Placed in reserve and laid up at Portsmouth in 1990 INTREPID was towed to the Mersey in 2008 to be broken up.

The Type 61 frigate HMS CHICHESTER pictured leaving Gibraltar. Built at Govan, she was completed in 1958 as one of four Salisbury class Aircraft Direction Frigates. In 1973 she was refitted for duties as a permanent Hong Kong guard ship, due in part to her good range conferred by her diesel machinery. Her Type 965 radar was removed and she was fitted with two extra 20mm Oerlikons and a single 40mm Bofors. She sailed for the colony later in that year and served there until 1976, returning to the UK to pay off into reserve before being broken up in 1981.

Built at Belfast by Harland and Wolff she was completed in 1965 as the commercial tanker EDENFIELD for Hunting (Eden) Tankers Ltd. Chartered and renamed RFA DEWDALE she is seen here outbound from Gibraltar in 1972. She was classed as a Mobile Bulk Tanker with very limited RAS capability. DEWDALE was one of three large tankers chartered by the MoD in 1967, for an initial period of seven years, to ensure fleet logistics support east of Suez. In 1973, whilst serving on the Beira Patrol she suffered a crankshaft seizure 50 miles south of Durban and was completely immobilised and drifting. She was towed to Durban, by RFA TARBATNESS, for repairs. In 1977 she was returned to her owners and reverted to her original name and was broken up in Taiwan in 1982.

The tug REWARD pictured leaving Portsmouth in June 1972. She was one of eight Bustler class Rescue Tugs completed during WW2 at the Henry Robb shipyard at Leith. Sister ship HESPERIA was a war loss. Most were sold off in the 1960's to Greek or Yugoslav commercial tug operators. REWARD was transferred to the RFA in 1963 and then the Port Auxiliary Service in 1970. In 1975 she was converted at Chatham for patrol duties, fitted with a 40mm gun and commissioned into the Royal Navy as HMS REWARD. On 10th August 1976, whilst operating as part of the Fishery Protection Squadron, she collided with a German containership in the Firth of Forth and sank. Raised a few weeks later, she was considered too badly damaged for further service and was sold and broken up near Inverkeithing.

RFA TIDEREACH is seen leaving Gibraltar in 1972 with the retiring Anglican Bishop taking passage to South Africa aboard her. Built by Swan Hunter and Wigham Richardson at their Wallsend yard she was completed in 1955, one of three Tide class replenishment oilers constructed for the Royal Fleet Auxiliary. They were the first purpose designed and built replenishment tankers for the Admiralty and incorporated lessons learned from WW2, especially operations with the Pacific Fleet Train and a need for a fast replenishment tanker that could keep up with a task force. RFA TIDEREACH was laid up for disposal in 1978 and on 16 March 1979 left Portsmouth under tow by the German Tug PETER WESSELS, bound for Bilbao, Spain, and breaking up.

RFA WAVE CHIEF entering Gibraltar harbour in 1972 with the Dog class tug AIREDALE alongside. WAVE CHIEF was built at Harland and Wolff's shipyard at Govan and launched as the EMPIRE EDGEHILL in 1946. Completed and renamed in the same year, she was one of a class of 20 tankers offered to the Admiralty during WW2. Performance varied considerably from ship to ship and the best eight were finally given an extensive refit, with extra accommodation added to the Bridge Deck and extra turbo cargo pumps and derricks to make them more satisfactory for Fleet work. WAVE CHIEF saw service during the Korean War and in 1959 was deployed to support RN units off Iceland during the 1st Cod War and again in 1973 during the 2nd Cod War. She was sold for breaking up in 1974.

The Tribal class Type 81 frigate HMS GURKHA displaying the half leader band on her forward funnel. Attached to the 7th Frigate Squadron and pictured arriving at Gibraltar in the spring of 1973 she was one of seven in the class. She was built by Thornycroft at their Woolston yard and completed in 1963. Serving in the Persian Gulf in the 1960's, as well as being involved during the Cod War with Iceland in 1976. She was fitted with variable depth sonar (VDS), along with one other of the class, but as a single screw ship the arrangement was not very satisfactory - her stern area looks extremely busy with 4.5-inch gun, winch and flight deck complete with Westland Wasp. She initially paid off into reserve in 1980 but recommissioned during 1982 to cover for ships deployed during the Falklands War. She paid off again in 1984 and was sold, along with two other units of her class, to Indonesia being renamed WILHELMUS ZAKARIAS YOHANNES.

HM Fleet Tender ASHCOTT comes alongside the North Mole at Gibraltar in 1973. Built by Plimbott in 1963, she was one of 14 Aberdovey class fleet tenders ordered for the Port Auxiliary Service. However, ASHCOTT was attached to HMS ROOKE Gibraltar and flew the white ensign. She was manned by crews from visiting navy guard ships on their monthly tours of duty at Gibraltar. ASHCOTT is a village in Somerset.

Seen at Gibraltar in 1973 is the Leander class frigate HMS JUNO, wearing the pennant number of her sister PHOEBE during filming for the BBC television series *Warship*. Several Leander's were used for the production of this fictional maritime story, PHOEBE being the original. JUNO, F 52 was built at Woolston by John I. Thornycroft and completed in 1967. In 1976 she was deployed off Iceland during the 3rd Cod War and was damaged when rammed by the gunboat TYR. In 1980 she joined NATOs Standing Naval Force Atlantic and in the same year was present at the Belgian Naval Review at Oostende. Converted in 1985 to a navigation training ship which saw the removal of most of her weapons. She was paid off in 1992 and was broken up in Spain in 1995.

The Helicopter Support Ship RFA ENGADINE approaching the south entrance at Gibraltar on 12th October 1973. Two Westland Sea King Helicopters are visible on her flight deck. Built by Henry Robb Ltd at Leith and completed in 1967 to provide initial at sea training for helicopter pilots. She was jointly manned by RN and RFA personnel and was able to accommodate 120 personnel, in addition to her crew, for flying training. In July 1969 she took part in the Western Fleet Review at Torbay along the aircraft carrier HMS EAGLE and 34 other warships of the Western Fleet. She was also deployed to the South Atlantic during the Falklands War. Laid up at Plymouth in 1989 and sold to Greek commercial interests in 1990. She was broken up on the beaches of Alang, India in 1996.

HMS MATAPAN pictured leaving Gibraltar in 1973 during her post refit trials. Originally a Battle class destroyer, she was built by John Brown on the Clyde and completed in 1947. After builders trials she was almost immediately laid up and would remain so until 1970 when converted at Portsmouth Dockyard to a Sonar Trials Ship. Emerging from refit she was unrecognisable, having a clipper bow, flush deck, an extra funnel, new bridge structure and a helicopter flight deck fitted. Below the waterline she had a bulbous bow and a deep skeg that increased her draught considerably. After machinery trials she was operated for the Admiralty Underwater Weapons Establishment (AUWE) at Portland. MATAPAN paid off in 1977 and was laid up in Portsmouth harbour. She was broken up at Blyth in 1979.

Built by Vickers-Armstrong at Barrow and completed in 1966, HMS VALIANT heads out into Gibraltar Bay in 1973. The second nuclear-powered submarine to be built for the Royal Navy and the first to have an all British propulsion system. She took part in the 1977 Silver Jubilee Fleet Review and was part of the Task Force sent to recapture the Falkland Islands in 1982, during which operation she transmitted more than 300 early air-warning alerts and spent 101 days on patrol off Argentina's Patagonian coast. She paid off in August 1994 and is currently (2016) laid up at Devonport Dockyard awaiting disposal.

An Eddy class coastal tanker RFA EDDYFIRTH, at Portsmouth in 1973. In all eight of this type were built, EDDYFIRTH at the Renfrew yard of Lobnitz ship-building, completing in 1954. They were designed to act as Fleet Attendant Oilers but, even as they were being built, their designed functions had become obsolete due to the rapid and widescale practice of refuelling at sea. They were reclassed as harbour and coastal tankers, moving fuel between bases and ships in port. EDDYFIRTH spent a large part of her career based at Malta, largely with the Motor Minesweeping Flotillas. In her latter years, she transported avcat and lubricating oils around the UK. She was the last of the class in service she decommissioned in 1981 and arrived at Seville, for breaking up, in March 1982.

Glasgow RNR division tender HMS CLYDE pictured at Portsmouth in 1974. She was built by Harland and Wolff at Belfast as HMS REPTON, one of the Ton class of Coastal Minesweepers, and completed in 1957. After service with the Vernon squadron she was towed to Gibraltar in 1967 and placed in reserve at Coaling Island minesweeper base. Commissioning as HMS CLYDE for the 10th MCMS in 1971, she served in that role until reverting to her original name in 1976. She saw service with the Fishery Protection Squadron for a short period in 1979 before finally paying off in 1980. She was sold to Pounds Ship Breakers at Portsmouth in 1982.

The submarine depot ship HMS DEFIANCE, built as HMS FORTH (*see page 52*), is seen in this 1974 picture berthed alongside at Devonport Dockyard. She remained in this role until 1978 when the new shoreside Fleet Maintenance Base was opened which assumed the name HMS DEFIANCE. Reverting to her original name, FORTH, the ship paid off in 1979 and was laid up at moorings on the Hamoaze, until sold for breaking up. She was scrapped on the Medway at Kingsnorth in 1985

The Armament Stores Carrier KINTERBURY sailing from Portsmouth in 1974. Built at Dartmouth by Philip and Son Ltd and completed in 1943 she was one of a pair, her sister ship being THROSK. Both saw WW2 service. She was operated by the Port Auxiliary Service which then became the RMAS in the mid 1970's. A regular visitor to Gibraltar she was always berthed at the far end of the South Mole, the berth designated for ships carrying dangerous cargo, after the fire and explosion aboard the ammunition ship BEDENHAM at the torpedo camber Gibraltar in 1951. In 1959 she was converted with hold stowage and with derricks for handling Sea Slug missiles for the trials ship HMS GIRDLE NESS. She was broken up by Liguria Maritime Ltd, Sittingbourne in 1978.

RFA RESOURCE moored to 'C' buoy in Plymouth Sound in 1974. Designated AFES or Ammunition, Food, Explosive Stores Ships, RESOURCE was built at Greenock by Scott's Shipbuilding and completed in 1967. Together with her sister, REGENT, they were affectionately known as 'Remorse' and 'Regret' and proudly boasted that they were designed to sink upright! She served in the Falklands and in the Adriatic at the time of the Balkan's conflict - she spent much of the mid 1990s in Split, Croatia, serving as a floating munitions storage for UN and IFOR troops in the former Yugoslavia. She was decommissioned in 1997 and in June that year was sold for £1.7 million to Harlequin Shipping Ltd and renamed RESOURCEFUL, sailing from Devonport bound for Indian breakers.

Built in 1970 by Vosper Thornycroft at their Camber Shipyard in Portsmouth as a private venture, TENACITY was purchased by the Royal Navy in 1972, after two periods of charter in 1971, and commissioned in 1973. She was fitted with three Proteus gas turbines giving her a speed of 40 knots, and two Paxman Ventura diesel engines for cruising. She was mainly employed as a member of the Fishery Protection Squadron, but also operated on anti-terror operations off Northern Ireland. She is pictured arriving at Portsmouth in 1974. She was sold to commercial interests in 1985 for conversion to a yacht but reportedly sank at her moorings. It has been reported that she was subsequently broken up in 2001.

First of the Type 21 frigates HMS AMAZON was completed by Vosper Thornycroft, Woolston, and is seen here outbound from the River Itchen shortly after commissioning in 1974. These ships were the RN's first privately designed warships for many years. They were also the first design to enter service with the RN to be
solely powered by gas-turbine engines. The class comprised eight ships, three being built by VT and the remaining five constructed at Glasgow by Yarrow and Co.
HMS AMAZON was the only one of the class not to take part in the Falkland's War. She was fitted with four Exocet missile launchers during a refit in the 1980's.
These were removed in 1993 when she was sold, along with the five other remaining ships of the class, to Pakistan where she serves (2016) as PNS BABUR.

Ton class Minesweeper HMS LALESTON was built by Harland and Wolff and completed in 1954. She was first attached to HMS VERNON and then later based at Portland with the 3rd MSS. She was converted during 1966-67 to a diving trials and training ship, here pictured off Southsea in 1974. During the refit her armament was removed as well as her minesweeping reel and loop. Her winch was replaced by a capstan and a decompression chamber was also added. She took part in the 1977 Silver Jubilee Fleet Review and by then her 40mm gun had been re-installed. In 1978 she became part of the 10th MSS and was allocated to the Ulster Division of the RNR. She was laid up in 1982 and scrapped in 1985.

Pictured near South Railway Jetty in 1974 is the 52.5ft harbour launch D23 built in 1965 at the Cowes yard of Groves and Gutteridge. One of a very large number of this type built over the years, they were mainly used as passenger ferries within the naval bases around the world but some were fitted with towing hooks for the movement of barges, pontoons etc. Several saw service at Gibraltar as pilot vessels. This picture shows D23 with a group of office staff enjoying a trip around Portsmouth dockyard.

The Torpedo Research and Trials ship RMAS WHITEHEAD leaving her base at Turnchapel Wharf near Plymouth in 1975. She was named after the 19th century engineer Robert Whitehead famous for his work in torpedo design. She was designed to provide mobile preparation, firing and control facilities for weapons and research vehicles. She also had equipment for tracking both weapons and targets and could analyse the results onboard. For firing torpedoes she was fitted with a triple Mk32 torpedo mounting on the upperdeck and a single 21-inch torpedo tube below the waterine in the bow. Built by Scotts Shipbuilding Co Ltd at Greenock she was completed in 1971 and, following decommissioning, sold to INCOM Ship Trading Ltd and broken up at Alang (India) in 1993.

HMS DITTISHAM, was a former Ham class Inshore Minesweeper, designed to operate in the shallow water of rivers and estuaries. She was built by the Fairlie Yacht Company and completed in 1954. She was placed in reserve, but in 1968 became a training tender to HMS GANGES at Shotley, transferring to HMS RALEIGH at Torpoint in 1973. In this 1976 picture she is seen at Plymouth Navy Days at the start of her river display. Disposed of by the Royal Navy in 1983 she became a training ship for the Kingston Sea Cadets, being renamed TS STEADFAST. She was finally broken up, being towed to Pounds at Portsmouth in April 1997. The ships of this class were all named after British villages, DITTISHAM being a small village in south Devon.

One of the WW2 built Tank Landing Ships Mk 3. LST 3523 was built in Canada and completed in 1945. She was commissioned as HMS TROUNCER in 1947. She was renamed the EMPIRE GULL in 1956 and transferred to the Atlantic Steam Navigation Company in that year. In 1961 she was operated for the Army by the British India Steam Navigation Company before transfer to the Royal Fleet Auxiliary in 1970. Her service with the RFA saw her based at Marchwood Military Port mainly carrying stores between the UK and northern Europe. She is pictured in 1976 leaving Portsmouth with the pennant number L3513. She paid off in 1978 and was broken up by Recuperaciones Submarinas S.A, Santander, Spain, in 1980.

HMS CYGNET was one of four Bird class patrol vessels built by Richard Dunston Ship builders at Hessle in the 1970's for the Royal Navy. She joined the Fishery Protection Squadron when completed and is seen leaving HMS VERNON on Christmas Day in 1976. These vessels proved to be poor seaboats and the design was considered unsuccessful. Two of the class were assigned as training tenders to Britannia Royal Naval College while the remaining pair, CYGNET and KINGFISH-ER, were assigned to the Northern Ireland Squadron. The Bird class were of a similar design to the Seal class long range recovery craft operated by the RAF's marine branch, one of which, HMAFV SEA OTTER, was transferred to the RN in 1985 and named HMS REDPOLE. CYGNET was decommissioned in 1996.

The Polaris submarine HMS REPULSE flies her paying off pennant after her only visit to Portsmouth pictured departing on 1st November 1976. She was en route from her base on the Clyde for refit at Rosyth dockyard. She was built at Barrow by Vickers Engineering Group, completed in 1968. REPULSE was the second of four Resolution class nuclear ballistic missile submarines (SSBN) built for the Royal Navy as part of the UK Polaris programme. Each submarine was armed with up to 16 Polaris A-3 nuclear missiles. At least one submarine was at sea on patrol at all times as part of the United Kingdom's continuous at-sea strategic nuclear deterrent. REPULSE was paid off in 1996 and is currently in storage at Rosyth.

Ordered by the Ghanaian government from Yarrows as a Presidential Yacht she was to have been named BLACK STAR. However, the order was cancelled before completion and she was laid up at Portsmouth. Taken over by the RN in 1972 she was refitted at Chatham Dockyard and later, in 1973, commissioned as HMS MERMAID. After work up she was deployed to the Far East and based at Singapore. She was photographed from the Round Tower, entering harbour in 1976. Later in that year whilst on exercise with the 10th MSS in the North Sea she collided with the minesweeper HMS FITTLETON which sank with loss of 12 lives. In 1977 she was sold to the Malaysian Navy and renamed HANG TUAH. In 1992 she was reclassified as a training ship and remains in service.

HMS NAIAD returns to Devonport in 1976 clearly showing the damage sustained to her bow after colliding with the Icelandic gunboat TYR during the 3rd Cod War. She was serving with the Fishery Protection Squadron at the time of this incident, as signified by the pendant displayed on her funnel. Built by Yarrow's at their Scotstoun yard and completed in 1965, she was modernized at Devonport between 1973-5. She emerged minus her 4.5-inch gun mounting which was replaced with the Australian Ikara anti-submarine missile system. She was at the Queen's Silver Jubilee Fleet Review in 1977 and in 1985 served with NATOs STANAVFORMED. In April 1987 she was decommissioned, and in 1989 was used as a static trials ship for hull vulnerability trials. In September 1990, she was sunk as a target.

RMAS PINTAIL, seen servicing the moorings at Falmouth in mid 1976, was one of the Wild Duck class mooring and salvage vessels that were operated in the UK and Mediterranean by the Royal Maritime Auxiliary Service . RMAS PINTAIL was built by Cammell Laird at Birkenhead and completed in 1964. She was based for most of her service life at Plymouth. In 1981 PINTAIL was involved in the salvage of the submarine HOLLAND 1 which sank off the Eddystone reef in 1913 whilst being towed to a breakers yard. PINTAIL was replaced in service by one of the larger Sal class vessels.

The aircraft carrier HMS ARK ROYAL pictured at the Silver Jubilee Fleet Review in June 1977. Photographed from the press ship RFA ENGADINE just after HMY BRITANNIA had steamed past with the royal party embarked. ARK ROYAL was laid down in 1943 at Birkenhead but not completed until 1955. One of four Audacious class carriers ordered. ARK ROYAL was to have been named IRRESISTIBLE. Two were cancelled in their early stages of construction at the end of WW2. Sister ship AUDACIOUS was completed as HMS EAGLE. ARK ROYAL paid off at Plymouth in early 1980 and was towed to Cairnryan for breaking up later in that year.

Pictured in the Solent during the fleet steam past on 29th June 1977, the day after the Silver Jubilee Review is the Tiger class helicopter cruiser HMS BLAKE. Built at the Fairfield Shipyard on the Clyde at Govan and was to have been named BELLEROPHON. She was completed in 1959 some 18 years after being laid down. Between 1965-9 she was converted at Portsmouth dockyard, emerging in her new role with a flight deck and hangar and capable of operating four Wessex helicopters which were replaced by the Westland Sea King HAS.1 helicopter in December 1972. In 1980 she was refitted again but on completion, due to man-power shortages, she became part of the Standby Squadron at Chatham. On 29 October 1982 she was towed from Chatham to Cairnryan for breaking up.

The oceangoing survey ship HMS HECLA with her Wasp Helicopter on the flight deck. She was photographed off Ryde, Isle of Wight on the 29th June 1977 after attending the Queen's Silver Jubilee Fleet Review. The name ship of a class of three Oceanographic vessels built for the Royal Navy by Yarrow and Company at their Blythswood yard. A further vessel of this type, SAS PROTEA, was built for the South African Navy. HECLA was completed in 1965. She saw service during the Falklands War as an ambulance/hospital ship, in which role she ferried wounded from both sides to the main hospital ship, SS UGANDA and then, following treatment, from UGANDA to Montevideo for repatriation. Sold in 1997 to commercial interests and renamed BLIGH, she was broken up in India 2004.

The Leander class frigate HMS PENELOPE pictured passing Drake's Island in Plymouth Sound in 1977. She was the main trials ship for the Sea Wolf missile system. Stripped of all her original armament in the 1960's, the launcher was fitted on her flight deck and associated director on a structure to the rear of her hangar. On completion of these trials she underwent an Exocet conversion as had CLEOPATRA (*see page 32*). In 1988 the ship suffered a machinery breakdown during replenishment operations with the Canadian tanker HMCS PRESERVER. The frigate suffered damage estimated in the millions. She paid off in 1991 and was sold to Ecuador and renamed PRESIDENTE ELOY ALFARO. PENELOPE had a long standing association with Gerry and Sylvia Anderson, the creators of the television series *Thunderbirds*.

Third of the six Swiftsure class fleet submarines SUPERB photographed in June 1977 outbound to the east from Spithead and the Silver Jubilee Fleet Review while taking part in the fleet steam past. Another vessel from the Vickers Shipbuilding Group at Barrow, she was launched on 30 November 1974 and commissioned on 13 November 1976. In 2001, she operated in the Indian Ocean in support of Operation Veritas, part of the War in Afghanistan. She was damaged after hitting a pinnacle while submerged in the Red Sea in 2008. She underwent temporary repairs at Souda Bay, Crete, before returning to the UK. After surveying the damage she was decommissioned earlier than planned and is laid up at Devonport Naval Base.

The inshore survey ship HMS WOODLARK, the former Ham class inshore minesweeper HMS YAXHAM, pictured after the Silver Jubilee Fleet Review in 1977. Built by J. Samuel White at Cowes on the Isle of Wight she was completed in March 1959. After service with the 50th MSS and then the 3rd she was converted to a survey vessel in 1964 and fitted with an enclosed bridge. She is seen here near the Nab Tower, on 28th June 1977. After service as a survey vessel she was operated by the Southampton University Royal Navy Unit as their training tender. In 1986 she was towed to Milford Haven to be used as a target.

The Type 42 destroyer GLASGOW photographed arriving at Portsmouth from her builders Swan Hunter in 1978, still flying the red ensign, prior to commissioning in 1979. GLASGOW was equipped with a twin Sea Dart missile launcher and a single Mk8 4.5-inch gun. A Westland Lynx helicopter was also carried. Whilst taking part in the Falklands War in 1982 she was hit by a bomb dropped by an Argentine Skyhawk. Although it did not explode, it passed clean through the aft engine room, damaging fuel systems and disabling the two Tyne cruise engines. On return to the UK she was repaired in Portsmouth dockyard. She was placed at extended readiness in 2002 but returned to the fleet in 2003 to replace her damaged sister NOTTINGHAM. Paying off finally in 2005 she was towed to Turkey for breaking up in 2009.

The Island class patrol vessel HMS ORKNEY seen in the Western Approaches on 13th October 1978 having sailed from Plymouth earlier that day. One of seven of this type, they were all built at Aberdeen by Hall Russell. They were largely employed on fishery protection duties but also operated in protection of UK off-shore installations. She was completed in 1977 and her duties could see her sail as far south as Gibraltar though visits to the Rock were normally for Rest and Recreation purposes. She was decommissioned in 1999 and laid up at Portsmouth. She was sold to the Trinidad and Tobago Defence Force in 2000 where she operated as TTS NELSON. She was withdrawn from service in 2015 when replaced by a newer vessel of the same name.

HMS SALISBURY, the name ship of the four, Type 61 air direction frigates. From 1961-62 she was modernised, receiving the large Type 965M radar, mounted a top a newly plated in mast. A further major modernisation saw the aft 40mm mounting replaced by a large deckhouse and the Sea Cat missile system. She was photographed in 1978 leaving Portsmouth under the white ensign and with a Royal Naval crew, bound for the eastern Mediterranean after it was reported that she had been sold to the Egyptian Navy. However, she returned to the UK as the sale did not go ahead. SALISBURY paid off into reserve and, from 1980-85 was employed as a harbour training ship at Devonport. In September 1985 she was towed out to sea and sunk as a target.

The Ton class Minesweeper HMS SHOULTON leaving Portsmouth in 1978. Built by the Montrose Shipbuilding Company, she was completed in 1955. She was converted in 1957 to an experimental minehunter at the Woolston yard of Vosper Thornycroft. At the same time her original Mirrlees engines were replaced with high speed Napier Deltic's. She was operated at Portland as a member of the 50th MSS by the Admiralty Underwater Weapons Establishment. In 1966 she was fitted with a Pump Jet Propulsion system, which today is in use worldwide in many high speed ferries, and a bow thruster. She also undertook trials with the French PAP unmanned minehunting system in 1972 at Brest. HMS SHOULTON was in attendance at the Queen's Silver Jubilee Fleet Review in June 1977. She was named after a village in Worcestershire. She paid off in 1979 and sold for scrapping, at Blyth, on 2 February 1981.

Photographed on 25th March 1979 is the aircraft carrier INVINCIBLE off Walney Island on the first day of builders sea trials. She was built at Barrow-in-Furness by Vickers Shipbuilding and Engineering, being laid down in 1973, launched on 3 May 1977 and commissioned on 11 July 1980. Following defence cuts it was announced that after several months of negotiations, the Australian government had agreed to buy the ship. However, following the invasion of the Falkland Islands that year, she was retained and formed an integral part of the Task Force deployed to recapture the islands. She was deployed to the Adriatic in 1993-5 at the time of the Balkan conflict. Decommissioned in 2005 she was laid up in Portsmouth Naval Base until towed to Aliaga in Turkey for breaking up in 2011.

The ill-fated Type 42 destroyer HMS COVENTRY here pictured outbound from Portsmouth in May 1979 during sea trials. Built by Cammell Laird at Birkenhead she was accepted from her builders in 1978. She is seen here without the radomes over her Type 909 directors, quite common during period of sea trial. Notice also the empty satellite communications platforms aft of the foremast. At this time such terminals were only fitted if the ship deployed. COVENTRY was part of the task group deployed to the South Atlantic in 1982 during the Falklands War. On 25th May 1982 she was sunk during an attack by Argentine aircraft. She was struck by three bombs, two of which penetrated the engine room opening the space to the sea. Within 20 minutes COVENTRY had been abandoned and had completely capsized.

The Type 21 frigate ARDENT is seen returning to Portsmouth on 18th June 1979 following participation in the Staff College Sea Days. Her Lynx helicopter can be seen on her flight deck and the Exocet launchers, fitted from build to later Type 21s, are clearly visible forward of the bridge. She was built by Yarrows and commissioned in 1977. ARDENT took part in the Falklands War, sailing from Devonport on 19 April 1982. On 22 May, whilst operating in Falkland Sound, she was attacked by Argentine Skyhawks. During the first raid she was straddled by two bombs which failed to explode. The next raid saw the ship hit by two bombs which exploded in the hangar and a third which entered a machinery space but failed to explode. A further raid saw her hit by four more bombs. With fires raging out of control the ship was abandoned. She sank the following morning. Her motto was 'Through Fire and Water'.

On 4th July 1979 pictured in Portsmouth dockyard is SRN6 Hovercraft 'ROMEO FOXTROT' being loaded on board RFA BACCHUS for shipment to Hong Kong. Together with her sister craft 'ROMEO JULIET', they were to be used for anti-illegal immigrant patrols in the waters around the colony. The hovercraft belonged to the Naval Hovercraft Trials Unit (formerly the Inter-service Hovercraft Trials Unit). Three types of hovercraft were operated by the unit, the large VT2, medium BH7 and the smaller SRN6. Based at HMS DAEDALUS at Lee-on-Solent, they were all fully amphibious and used on fleet exercises and a variety of trials ranging from logistics support to mine countermeasures. The three SRN6 hovercraft were all withdrawn from service by 1984.

Name ship of a class of three, the Fast Training Boat SCIMITAR is shown being loaded aboard the heavy lift ship HAPPY PIONEER at Portland on 7th August 1979 for shipment to Hong Kong where she would be based and used in the control of illegal immigrants. She was a guard ship during the 1977 Fleet Review at Spithead. Built by Vospers in 1970 the three vessels were a development of the Brave class and were operated by the Fast Training Boat Squadron. Unarmed, they were used in the training role to give the Fleet more experience of the capabilities of fast, modern attack craft, then becoming available to potential enemies. SCIMITAR returned to the UK in 1981 and paid off in 1982 for disposal. She was sold to Greek interests in 1983 and renamed AQUILON.

Off Portland during Flag Officer Sea Training (FOST) 'Thursday War', the Fast Training Boat HMS SABRE photographed in the summer of 1979 from her sister CUTLASS at her full speed of 40 knots. During the Silver Jubilee Fleet Review in 1977 all three of the class were used to patrol the review area. HMS SABRE collided with a breakwater at Alderney in the Channel Islands whilst on a courtesy visit in July 1980 losing her bow. Towed back to Portsmouth and laid up, she was nicknamed 'HMS BOWLESS' and was placed on the disposal list in 1982.

Leaving her Portsmouth base is the first of the Type 42 destroyers SHEFFIELD in the spring of 1980. Built by Vickers Shipbuilding group at Barrow she was damaged during construction by an explosion. The damaged section of hull was replaced with that from an identical ship, HERCULES, being built for the Argentine Navy. SHEFFIELD was commissioned on 28th February 1975 and became the first British loss during the Falklands campaign when, on 4th May 1982, she was hit by an air launched Exocet missile launched from an Argentine Super Etendard. Initially it was believed that the missile failed to explode but a report in 2015 concluded that it did. Fires raged throughout the ship and she was abandoned. She was taken in tow by YARMOUTH but, enroute to South Georgia, she sank in heavy seas on 10th May.

First of the Glass Reinforced Plastic-hulled Hunt class Mine Counter Measures Vessels, HMS BRECON was photographed off Portland on 13th March 1980 during a press day. Built by Vosper Thornycroft at their Woolston yard she was handed over to the Royal Navy at the end of 1979 for service with the 1st MCM squadron based at Rosyth. During her career she carried out mine clearance in the aftermath of the Falklands War along with her sister HMS LEDBURY. She also deployed east of Suez during the Gulf War in 1991. In 1998 she became a patrol vessel attached to the Northern Ireland Squadron. BRECON decommissioned in 2005, and in 2008 she became a static training ship for new recruits at HMS RALEIGH.

At anchor off Ryde on 13th May 1980 is the Leaf class replenishment tanker RFA BRAMBLELEAF. Laid down and launched as the commercial tanker HUDSON DEEP at the Birkenhead yard of Cammell Laird, she was one of four STaT 32 type tankers ordered by Hudson Fuel and Shipping but due to financial difficulties they were unable to accept the ships. HUDSON DEEP was bareboat chartered by the MoD and completed for RFA service, with additional accommodation and replenishment rigs, in February 1980 as BRAMBLELEAF. Coincidentally her pennant Number A81 is the same as her predecessor which was sold out of RFA service in 1972. The ship was purchased by MoD(N) in February 1983, serving until 2007. She was scrapped by Van Heyghen Freres at Ghent, Belgium, where she arrived on 20th August 2009.

During Staff College Sea Days the Leander class frigate HMS DIOMEDE breaks away from the Type 21 frigate HMS AMAZON. She was photographed on 9th June 1980 from RFA OLMEDA which was the dedicated press ship. AMAZON's Lynx helicopter is clearly visible on her deck. HMS DIOMEDE was built at the Scotstoun yard of Yarrows and completed in April 1971. She saw service during the second and third Cod Wars whilst serving with the Fishery Protection Squadron and was badly damaged following a collision with the gunboat TYR and two with BALDUR. In the 1970's she was one of the Leanders used in the filming of *Warship*, the television series. Never converted, she decommissioned in 1988 and was sold to Pakistan, where she served as PNS SHAMSHER.

The County class destroyer NORFOLK pictured in June 1980 during Staff College Sea Days. A Type 21 frigate is visible through the haze. NORFOLK was built by Swan Hunter at their Wallsend yard, as was her older sister LONDON. A total of eight Counties made up the class. NORFOLK was completed in 1970. Four Exocet missile launchers were fitted in place of her 'B' turret during a refit in 1972. Three more of the class received this missile system. She represented the RN at the Belgian Naval Review at Oostende in 1980. She was sold to Chile in 1982 and left Portsmouth on 17th February 1982 flying her paying off pennant for delivery to her new owners. Handed over in Chile and renamed CAPITÁN PRAT she was rebuilt as a helicopter carrier in 2001. Laid up in 2006 she was scrapped in Mexico in 2008.

HMS SPEEDY photographed near the Nab Tower on 28th July 1980. Purchased 'off the shelf' from her builders Boeing at Seattle in the US, she was shipped to the UK and fitted out to suit MoD requirements by Vosper Thornycroft. She was ordered in 1978 to evaluate the offshore oil and fishery protection roles where the RN could use her unique capabilities of high speed and extreme manoeuvrability. She served with the Fishery Protection Squadron and as a patrol vessel in the North Sea oilfields - she also undertook minesweeping trials. Although she achieved success in the fishery protection role due to her high speed, she was limited by sea state and range. Ultimately she was found not to be suitable for RN requirements and was paid off in 1982 and laid up. She was sold in 1986.

During annual sea training ALFRISTON is photographed on 31st August 1980 just ahead of the Leander class frigate DIOMEDE on the moorings below Britannia Royal Naval College at Dartmouth. At the time ALFRISTON was tender to HMS WESSEX, the Royal Naval Reserve division at Southampton. Built at the Woolston yard of John I. Thornycroft and completed in 1954, she spent most of her career as an RNR tender. Firstly she took the name WARSASH based at Southampton. Then in 1960 she served for the reserves at Belfast as KILMOREY. In 1975 returning to RN service she became a member of the Fishery Protection Squadron under her original Ton class name. As a member of the FPS she took part in the Silver Jubilee Review. In January 1979 she returned to Southampton as tender to HMS WESSEX before paying off in 1986. She was broken up at Bruges, Belgium in 1988. Alfriston is a village in East Sussex.

On 21st January 1981 HMS HERMES is seen in the tidal basin at Portsmouth dockyard attended by several tugs and still in dockyard hands during the refit which would see her emerge with her new 'ski jump'. Built by Vickers Armstrong and laid down in 1944, construction was suspended in 1945. Work was resumed in 1952 to clear the slipway and the hull was launched on 16 February 1953. The vessel was completed in 1959 after extensive modifications which included installation of a Type 984 'searchlight' 3D radar, a fully angled deck with a deck-edge elevator, and steam catapults. In 1972 she was refitted to serve as a helicopter carrier in the amphibious assault role and by 1976 had once again been re-roled as an ASW carrier. After her 1981 refit she was once again able to operate fixed wing aircraft, in the shape of the Sea Harrier, and served as the Flagship of the Task Force sent to liberate the Falklands in 1982. In 1984 she paid off and in 1986 was sold to the Indian Navy where she served as INS VIRAAT until decommissioning in 2016.

RMAS BARBARA, one of eight 'girl' class tugs. She was built at Hessle by Richard Dunston and completed in 1963. Initially based at Rosyth then transferred to Chatham in 1967. She was photographed in the Medway in April 1981. These tugs were, reportedly, very powerful for their size and, with full power applied on a heavy pull, the sterns had a habit of coming awash. Most of the class were disposed of in the early 1980's. Two were transferred to the MoD (Army) for use at Marchwood Military Port.

A former commercial trawler, HMS VENTURER photographed during exercise Ocean Safari on 16th September 1981. Built at the Woolwich shipyard of Cubow Ltd as the stern trawler SUFFOLK MONARCH she was completed for her Lowestoft owners in 1973. Chartered in 1978 by the MoD along with her sister ship SUFFOLK HARVESTER, which was named HMS ST. DAVID, both joined the 10th MSS. HMS VENTURER was allocated to the RNR as tender to the Bristol Division and HMS ST. DAVID to South Wales at Cardiff. Both were equipped to refine the concept of EDATS - Extra Deep Armed Team Sweep. Operating as a pair, they towed a sweep between them that followed the profile of the bottom and cut the mooring wires of the mines; these released mines would then be destroyed on the surface with gunfire. The system went on to equip the River class employed by the RNR. Both ships were decommissioned and returned to their owners in 1983.

The minelayer ABDIEL operating as support ship to the 10th MSS with CROFTON alongside during exercise Rockhaul. She was photographed from on board ALFRISTON at the port of Syracuse in Sicily on 8th May 1982. ABDIEL was built at the Woolston yard of John I. Thornycroft and completed in 1967. She was designated by the MoD as an 'exercise minelayer' and her official role was to train RN personnel in minelaying operations using test/dummy naval mines, not to lay offensive mines operationally, although the ability to lay practice minefields would suggest an ability to lay an offensive minefield as well. In 1974 she was headquarters ship during mine clearance operations in the Suez Canal working with ships from the 2nd MSS based at HMS VERNON. Disposed of in 1988, she was towed to Spain and broken up at Santander in the same year.

The Type 42 destroyer HMS EXETER at anchor near Ryde on 28th July 1982 on her return from the South Atlantic and action during the Falkland's War. Built by Swan Hunter, Tyne & Wear she was completed in 1980. She was the first of the Batch 2 Type 42s and embodied better sensors, such as the Type 1022 radar in place of the older Type 965 'bedstead' aerial, and a slightly revised internal layout. In this picture it shows her with her pennant number erased and a large black band painted from the boot topping through her hull to the top of her funnel so as to distinguish her from the pair of Type 42 destroyers operated by Argentina. She also had a turquoise hull on and below the waterline; this was an experimental co-polymer paint which was only available in a few non-standard colours at the time. EXETER also served in the First Gulf War in 1991. In 2008 she was placed at extended readiness and paid off in 2009. She was towed to Aliaga, Turkey in 2011 for breaking up by Leyal Ship Recycling.

The Survey ship HMS HECLA at Plymouth on 29th July 1982. She is pictured returning from service during the Falklands War where she operated as an ambulance ship having been converted for this role at Gibraltar dockyard. The Queen's Harbour Master escorts her up the Tamar. For the role she was painted overall white, including mast, funnel and cranes and had prominent red crosses on the hull, funnel and bridge front. Her Wasp helicopter, used to transport casualties between hospital ships and ambulance ships, was also adorned with red crosses in white boxes. To abide by the Geneva Convention on hospital ships, all classified material and equipment was landed and Marisat, a commercial communications satellite, installed. The White Ensign was lowered and the Union Flag and the Red Cross flag flown at the mainmast.

When Argentina invaded the Falklands in 1982 thoughts turned to how to counter any mine threat. The RN's mine warfare capability was purely coastal, the Ton-class minesweepers, with a range of around 2,300 nm would be totally unsuitable for either the distance or the conditions. The answer was to charter civilian vessels. PICT was built by Brooke Marine at their Lowestoft yard in 1973 for British United Trawler's Finance of Hull as the stern trawler and was taken over, along with four similar ships, in April 1982. They were converted to EDATS minesweepers; commissioned into the RN and sailed as the 11th MCMS later in April 1982 for duties in and around the Falkland Islands. On the surrender of Argentine forces the ships were ordered to Port Stanley to clear the approaches to the harbour. PICT was photographed on 11th August on the squadron's return to the Firth of Forth. She was returned to her owners later that month. She was broken up in India in 2005 under the name FRIENDSHIP.

The Ice Patrol Ship HMS ENDURANCE departs Portsmouth for the South Atlantic on 15th November 1982. This was her first return to the Falklands since the Islands were recaptured earlier that year. She is pictured off Fountain Lake Jetty escorted by the Queen's Harbour Master, 'The Red Plum' looking very smart in the autumn sunshine. She was built in West Germany, at Rendsburg, for Danish ship owners Lauritzen Line in 1956 as the ice strengthened cargo ship ANITA DAN. Purchased by the MoD in 1967 she was converted at Belfast by Harland and Wolff, commissioning in the following year as a replacement for the 1936 built HMS PROTECTOR (*see page 6*). She paid off in 1991 and was broken up in Pakistan during 1993.

HMS ILLUSTRIOUS returns to Portsmouth from the South Atlantic. Photographed from a Sea King Helicopter, seen approaching the harbour entrance on 8th December 1982 and looking very smart with her crew at Procedure Alpha. She was built by Swan Hunter as the second of the Invincible class. She was commissioned, at sea, on 20 June 1982 and, after storing at Portsmouth, left hurriedly for the South Atlantic on 2nd August to relieve HERMES and INVINCIBLE. After the Falklands War, she was deployed on Operation Southern Watch in Iraq, then Operation Deny Flight in Bosnia during the 1990s and Operation Palliser in Sierra Leone in 2000. Following the retirement of the Harrier in 2010 she operated as a helicopter carrier. She paid off in 2014 and is laid up (2016) in Portsmouth naval base.

RFA SIR LAMORAK, a roll-on-roll-off ferry built in Norway in 1972 as the M/V ANU and chartered by the MoD as a temporary replacement for the SIR GALA-HAD lost during the Falklands War. ANU had four subsequent names before becoming the LAKESPAN ONTARIO in 1981. She commissioned into the Royal Fleet Auxiliary in March 1983. The photograph was taken in the Solent as she approached Outer Spit Buoy on 3rd March prior to entering Portsmouth dockyard. She was mainly employed in the transport of supplies for the military from Marchwood on Southampton water to northern Europe. She was returned to her owners in 1986 and renamed MERCHANT TRADER. Receiving five further names in due course she could be seen trading Portsmouth to the Channel Islands as the PRIDE OF PORTSMOUTH and later as NORMAN COMMODORE before going to Finnish owners in 1996 as the FJARDVAGEN. She is still (2016) operating in the Gulf of Bothnia, a veteran of some 43 years of service.

During Staff College Sea Days on 26th May 1983 the Type 21 Frigate HMS ALACRITY is seen off the Isle of Wight. Built at Yarrow's she was completed just in time to attend the Silver Jubilee Fleet Review in June 1977, together with three of her sister ships. In 1980 she was deployed to the Far East and was one of a group of RN ships to sail up the Yangtse river, the first to do so since AMETHYST. She saw action during the Falklands campaign and during a night transit of Falkland Sound, encountered and sank the Argentine transport ship ISLA DE LOS ESTADOS. She paid off in 1994 and was sold for further service to the Pakistani Navy where she was renamed PNS BADR and fitted with Chinese LY 60N missiles in place of the Exocet. She was paid off in 2014.

The inshore survey vessel HMS ECHO in Plymouth sound on 31st August 1983. Together with EGERIA and ENTERPRISE, she was one of three 'E' class built on the hull design of the Ham class Inshore Minesweepers. Built for coastal and harbour hydrographic survey operations she had two echo sounding machines and sonar for wreck location. All three were based at Chatham. ECHO was built by J. Samuel White at Cowes and commissioned on 12 September 1958. She was sold in 1985.

Seen passing HMS ILLUSTRIOUS in the Hamoaze, the nuclear powered submarine HMS TRAFALGAR arrives at Plymouth on 31st August 1983. She was built by VSEL at Barrow-in-Furness and commissioned in May of that year. This was her inaugural visit to her home port being based at HMS DEFIANCE in Devonport dock-yard. TRAFALGAR was the first in a class of seven nuclear attack submarines completed in the 1980's, a development of the earlier Swiftsure class. She was the first RN submarine to launch Tomahawk cruise missiles against Afghanistan during Operation Veritas in 2002 and returned to Plymouth flying the traditional 'Jolly Roger' signifying a successful combat patrol. She decommissioned on 4 December 2009 and is in long term storage at Devonport Naval Base.

Built as the 'ISLAS MALVINAS' for the Argentine Coast Guard, this vessel was one of a class of twenty such Z-28 class vessels built for Argentina by Blohm & Voss of Hamburg, Germany, all of which entered service in 1978. During the Falklands War she was seized by crew from the Type 42 destroyer HMS CARDIFF and locally commissioned as HMS TIGER BAY. She was used as a despatch ship operating between ships at anchor and the shore. She was transported to Portsmouth naval base arriving on 8th September 1983 onboard the semi-submersible M/V DYVI SWAN and was unloaded in the Solent along with the damaged RCT landing craft ANTWERP. After being laid up TIGER BAY was sold in June 1986.

The leader of the Dartmouth Training Squadron, also known at the time as the 6th Frigate Squadron was HMS PLYMOUTH, a Rothesay class Type 12M frigate seen together with her sister ship HMS LONDONDERRY also of the 6th FS. The ships were photographed on captains manoeuvres in the English Channel during January 1984 prior to the squadrons departure to the West Indies. HMS PLYMOUTH was built at Devonport Dockyard and completed in 1961. HMS LONDONDERRY was built at the Cowes yard of J. Samuel White on the Isle of Wight and completed in 1960. HMS PLYMOUTH was in attendance at the Queen's Silver Jubilee Fleet Review in 1977 and saw action during the Falklands War in 1982. Paying off in 1988 she was displayed as a visitor attraction in several ports throughout the UK. Lately moored at Birkenhead she was sold for scrap and towed to Turkey for breaking up in 2014. HMS LONDONDERRY saw service in the West Indies in the 1960's and also visited Argentina. She was a member of the Atlantic NATO squadron in 1973. In 1975 she underwent conversion at Rosyth dockyard to a trials ship for ASWE at Portland, emerging four years later with her armament removed and fitted with two additional masts. The photograph shows her with one extra mast. She was finally decommissioned at the end of her West Indies trip on 29th March 1984 and became a static training ship attached to HMS SULTAN at Gosport. In June 1989 she was sunk as a target.

The seabed operations vessel HMS CHALLENGER shows her versatility to the world's press in August 1984. She was ordered from Shipbuilders Scott Lithgow at Greenock as a replacement for the chartered M/V SEAFORTH CLANSMAN. She was completed in 1984 as the Royal Navy's first purpose built ship able to support saturation diving to great depths. A moonpool amidships allowed the deployment of a diving bell from which divers could transfer to a decompression chamber and thereby remain under pressure ready to dive again. An 'A' frame at the stern allowed for the deployment of submersibles. However, by 1990 she was laid up, seen as being a very expensive piece of kit which the MoD could not afford. She was sold off and converted for the recovery of diamonds from the sea bed off the coast of Namibia, a role in which she continues to operate (2016) as YA TOIVO.

HMS KENT was one of eight County class destroyers built for the Royal Navy and all completed between 1963 and 1970. She was constructed at the Belfast shipyard of Harland and Wolff, one of four Batch 1 County class. None of the Batch 1 class received Exocet missiles and all had very short careers. She was decommissioned in 1980 and became a static training ship moored at Whale Island in Portsmouth Harbour. She was photographed on 30th October 1984 being towed out of Portsmouth by the tug ROYSTERER for a conversion, at Devonport, to a training ship for the Sea Cadet Corps. She remained in this role, at Portsmouth, until 1993 when replaced by BRISTOL. KENT was sold for scrap in 1997 and removed from Portsmouth by the Russian tug AGAT, bound for breaking up in India.

En route to Hong Kong HMS SWALLOW photographed on 4th November 1984 arriving at Portsmouth from her builders Hall Russell at Aberdeen. One of five Peacock class patrol boats all built at Aberdeen as replacements for the five Ton class minesweepers that made up the Hong Kong Patrol Squadron since 1971. They were the only RN ships to be equipped with the Oto-Melara 76mm compact gun. In 1988 SWALLOW, and her sister SWIFT, were sold to the Irish Naval Service, SWALLOW being commissioned as LÉ CIARA. When Hong Kong was handed back to China in 1997 at the end of the 99 year lease, the remaining three vessels of the Peacock class were sold to the Philippine government for service with their navy.

The Broad-beamed Leander class frigate HMS JUPITER photographed leaving Portsmouth on 4th March 1985. At this time she was attached to the 8th Frigate Squadron. Built by Yarrows at Scotstoun she was first commissioned for service with the Royal Navy in August 1969. She saw service in the West Indies in the early 1970's and was another of the class to be used in the filming of *Warship*. In 1980 she upgraded to carry the Seawolf missile system. Her twin 4.5-inch gun turret was removed and replaced by four MM38 Exocet missiles and a sextuple Seawolf missile launcher forward. Such were the weight considerations associated with the new missiles and their systems that much topweight had to be removed. The superstructure and mainmast were significantly reduced in size and even the funnel cap was removed. In 1986 she was deployed to the Persian Gulf and served on the Armilla Patrol. She decommissioned in 1992 and was broken up at Alang in India six years later.

HMS ITCHEN was one of 12 River class minesweepers built by Richards at their Lowestoft shipyard as replacement vessels for the ageing Ton class minesweepers operated by the RNR. She was photographed arriving at Portsmouth on 27th July 1985 and commissioned for Southampton RNR unit as a member of the 10th MCMS on 12th October 1985. The class was designed for the Extra Deep Armed Team Sweep (EDATS) system. No influence sweep equipment was carried. HMS BLACKWATER was never allocated for RNR use but saw service with the RN as a Fishery Protection Vessel. After RNR service ORWELL had her sweep gear removed and was attached to the Dartmouth Training Squadron. Likewise ARUN and SPEY were allocated to the Northern Ireland Squadron on paying off from the reserves. All were eventually sold off, seven seeing further service with the Brazilian Navy, four commissioned into the Bangladeshi Navy and one went to Guyana. HMS ITCHEN was named BRACUI upon her sale to Brazil in 1998.

The rebuilt Landing Ship Logistic RFA SIR TRISTRAM photographed leaving Portsmouth on 13th October 1985. She was built on the Tyne by Hawthorn Leslie and completed in 1967. Two more of the class, SIR BEDIVERE and SIR PERCIVALE, were also constructed by Hawthorn Leslie. During the Falklands campaign she was attacked by Argentine A-4 Skyhawks on 8th of June at Fitzroy Creek, just south of Bluff Cove. She was hit by three bombs and fires started in the steering flat, above which were pallets of ammunition. The ship was abandoned and her crew evacuated to HMS FEARLESS. At the end of the conflict the wreck was returned to the UK aboard the semi-submersible heavy lift ship DAN LIFTER for rebuilding, returning to RFA service in 1985. In 1991 she took part in the 1st Gulf War and in 2003 provided alongside support to British Forces in Sierra Leone. She paid off in 2005 and in 2007, following conversion work at Falmouth, arrived at Portland, where she is used as Training Ship for Maritime Special Forces, replacing the former escort maintenance ship RAME HEAD.

RMAS ROBUST, one of three large Roysterer class tugs built for the MoD in the early 1970's is seen at Portsmouth in this 17th March 1986 image. She was towing the aircraft carrier HMS HERMES to Devonport where she would be refitted for service with the Indian Navy. ROBUST was completed in 1974 by Charles D. Holmes at their shipyard at Beverley on the Humber. Designed for ocean towage and salvage she could also be employed for use within the naval bases as a harbour berthing tug. ROBUST was based for some of her career at Gibraltar as well as Devonport. All three of the 'R's were used to tow the old aircraft carrier ARK ROYAL from Plymouth to the ship breakers yard at Cairnryan in Scotland on 22nd September 1980.

The submarine tender HMS WAKEFUL, based at HMS NEPTUNE, Faslane on the Gareloch. She is pictured arriving at Portsmouth on 20th March 1986. Built for Swedish owners at Selby by Cochranes Ship builders and completed as the tug HERAKLES, she was renamed DAN in 1968, still operating under Swedish registry. In 1974 she was purchased by the MoD and commissioned as WAKEFUL and initially allocated to the Fishery Protection Squadron, until sufficient Island class OPVs were available. As well as providing submarine security on the Clyde she also acted on occasion as a submarine target vessel. She was replaced by SENTINEL in 1987 and, after paying off she was sold to Greek operators in 1988 and renamed AEGEAN PELAGOS. She was still in service in 2016.

RFA RELIANT in Plymouth Sound on 27th May 1986. She was built in Poland at the Gdansk Shipyard as the MV ASTRONOMER for Harrisons of London and completed in 1977 as a Ro/Ro Container ship. One of the STUFT ships (Ship Taken Up From Trade) she was converted as an aircraft transport having a hangar and flight deck fitted for service during the Falklands War. At the end of 1982 she was chartered by MoD and, during an extensive refit, was fitted with the ARA-PAHO aircraft handling system. She was commissioned as RFA RELIANT and saw service, firstly during the evacuation of the multinational force from Lebanon in 1984 and then going south again to the Falklands, before heading back to the UK in 1986 where she was decommissioned and sold off to private owners. She resumed her mercantile career, firstly as MV ADMIRALTY ISLAND, then renamed MV WEALTHY RIVER in 1989, before going for scrap in India during 1998.

Name ship of the class of diesel electric patrol submarines HMS OBERON is pictured paying off for disposal at Portsmouth on 10th December 1986. The submarine HMS WALRUS, one of the Porpoise class also returned to her base at HMS DOLPHIN to decommission on the same day. The Oberon class were a very successful UK post-war design, variants of which served with the navies of Australia, Brazil, Canada and Chile. OBERON was built at Chatham Dockyard and commissioned in 1961 as the first of 13 such submarines for the Royal Navy. She was sold in 1987 to the Seaforth Group to be refitted for resale to Egypt but the deal fell through and she was broken up at Grimsby in 1991

One of the Churchill class nuclear powered submarines, HMS CONQUEROR is seen on 9th March 1987 leaving 40 Berth in the Port of Southampton after a courtesy visit. British nuclear submarines have been regular visitors to Southampton. Built by Cammell Laird at Birkenhead on the Wirral, she was first commissioned in 1971. She saw service during the Falklands War where she became the only nuclear-powered submarine known to have engaged an enemy ship with torpedoes, sinking the Argentine cruiser GENERAL BELGRANO on 2nd May 1982. CONQUEROR paid off in 1990 and is currently in long term storage in Devonport dockyard, although her periscopes, captain's cabin and main control panel from the manoeuvring room are on display in the Royal Navy Submarine Museum in Gosport.

Attached to HMS RALEIGH for new entry training, HM Ships MANLY, MENTOR and MILBROOK are seen here during a 'jackstay transfer' exercise in Torbay on 17th February 1983. All three were built at Dunston's shipbuilders in 1982. Very similar in design to the Clovelly class fleet tenders operated by various departments including RN, RM, RNXS and RMAS, although fitted with a larger wheelhouse and bridge and a full beam structure for the wardroom, galley and dining room. The training ships would take out Seamanship trainees from Raleigh for a week at a time with short trips along the south coast. On occasion there would be a requirement to take classes of overseas navigation officers to sea for practical training. A fourth vessel, MESSINA was operated by the Royal Marines. All were discarded in 1991.

The small fleet tanker RFA BLACK ROVER refuels the Batch 1 Type 22 frigate HMS BATTLEAXE and the Leander class frigate HMS ARETHUSA during exercise 'Spring Train' in the western Atlantic near to Gibraltar. The photograph was shot from HMS BATTLEAXEs Lynx helicopter on 20th April 1983. This was the first major exercise conducted after the Falklands campaign, some dozen HM Ships and Royal Fleet Auxiliaries taking part. The Rover class could transfer fuel oils and limited supplies of other naval stores. For RAS tasking, they could refuel a vessel on either beam, as here, and a third over the stern. Although not equipped with a flight of their own, the large flight deck allowed vertical replenishment (VERTREP) using the receiving ships helicopters.

On exercise in Southampton water HMS HUNTER photographed from her sister HMS FENCER on 26th May 1983. HUNTER was one of five Attacker class patrol vessels built at the yard of Fairey Allday Marine near Southampton. Completed in 1983, she was attached to London division of the RNR as one of the university tenders, but based at HMS WESSEX in Southampton. Latterly she formed the Cyprus Squadron, with sisters ATTACKER and STRIKER, stationed on the island to provide support to the UK Sovereign Base Area. She was withdrawn from service in 1991 and, together with the rest of the class, was sold to the Lebanese Navy in 1992 where she served as BEIRUT.

HMS CORNWALL the first of the Batch 3 Type 22 frigates to be completed arriving at Portsmouth from her builders Yarrow's of Glasgow on 19th February 1988. During a television interview prior to her arrival in Portsmouth, a reference had been made that she had more fire power than a WW2 cruiser, a bit 'tongue in cheek'. Hence the reason for her pennant number C 99 which was formerly that of the Tiger class cruiser HMS BLAKE. She is seen flying her builders house flag and was under the red ensign. She was accepted later that day and was commissioned on 23rd April 1988 at Falmouth. She paid off at Plymouth on 25th April 2011. After lay up in Devonport she was moved to Portsmouth along with her three sister ships. After a further lay up period she was towed from Portsmouth on 24 October 2013 bound for breaking up by Swansea Drydocks Ship Recycling in Wales.

Photographed off Southsea on 26th February 1988 approaching Outer Spit Buoy is RFA SIR GALAHAD. This was her first visit to Portsmouth naval base. She was built by Swan Hunter at their yard on the Tyne as a replacement for the earlier ship of that name that was lost during the Falklands War. Completed in 1987 she was given the same pennant number as her predecessor. She differed from the earlier LSL's in as much as she was fitted with a bow visor, instead of the side-opening bow doors, and a 22 tonne capacity scissor lift amidships. She operated in the Gulf during both Gulf Wars and was the first ship to enter Umm Qasr, with humanitarian aid, in March 2003. She paid off into reserve in 2006 and was sold to the Brazilian Navy the following year where she serves as NdCC GARCIA D'AVILA.

RFA ARGUS, built in Italy at Marghera, near Venice, and completed in 1981 as the Ro/Ro container ship M/V CONTENDER BEZANT, and registered in Bermuda. She is seen arriving at Portsmouth in March 1988. Taken up from trade by the MoD in 1982, she saw service in the South Atlantic transporting military supplies for use by British forces during the Falklands War. She was purchased in 1984 from her owners and converted to an Aviation Training Ship at Belfast completing in 1987. First commissioned for her new role as an RFA in June 1988, she went on to see service in the Gulf war as a Casualty Receiving Ship and was also deployed to the Adriatic during the Balkan conflict in the 1990's. In 2009 she was modernised and her primary role was changed to that of Casualty Receiving ship, being equipped with extensive medical facilities. In 2014 she was deployed to assist with the Ebola outbreak in Sierra Leone, West Africa.

HMS REDPOLE was formerly named HMAFV SEA OTTER and operated by the Royal Air Force. She is seen leaving Portsmouth on 20th June 1988. Built by Fairmile at Berwick-upon-Tweed she was completed for the RAF Marine Branch in 1970 as a Long Range Recovery and Support Craft and transferred for Royal Naval service in 1984. Renamed REDPOLE she joined the Northern Ireland Squadron until replaced by HMS ARUN in 1994. For operations off Northern Ireland she was painted dark grey. She was placed on the disposal list and in 1996 was sold to private owners and operated as the BADTZ MARU - very little changed from her RN days - she even retained her unusual navigation lighting which enabled her to display deceptive combinations of running lights at night!

The Leander class frigate HMS ARETHUSA enters Portsmouth harbour on 4th April 1989 flying her paying off pennant. At the time she was attached to the 7th Frigate Squadron. Built at Cowes on the Isle of Wight by J. Samuel White, she was completed in 1965. ARETHUSA and seven of her sister ships were converted in the mid 1970's to carry the Australian designed Ikara anti-submarine weapon, her conversion taking place at Chatham Dockyard. This saw the removal of her twin 4.5-inch gun and Type 965 radar. During a refit in 1985 she was fitted with towed array sonar, the reel of which can be seen at her stern - she was the only Ikara conversion to be so fitted. After her decommissioning she was laid up at Portsmouth until 1st June 1991 when she was towed from Portsmouth by the tug RMAS ROLLICKER and used as a target.

The 'O' class submarine HMS OSIRIS returns to her base at HMS DOLPHIN, home of the 1st Submarine Squadron, on 8th September 1989 showing her new bow sonar. She was commissioned into the Royal Navy in 1964 after construction by Vickers Armstrong. Along with several of her sister ships, she took part in the Silver Jubilee Fleet Review in June 1977. In 1982, during the Falklands campaign, she was employed on minelaying work in the South Atlantic. She decommissioned late in 1989 and was sold to the Canadian Forces to provide spares for their own Oberon class boats. She was towed to Cammell Lairds, Birkenhead, who completed the stripping out of essential equipment. She was finally broken up on the Mersey in 1992.

With her crew lining the deck and paying off pennant streamed HMS EURYALUS enters Portsmouth harbour for the last time in April 1989, on the same day as her sister ARETHUSA. EURYALUS was built by Scotts Shipbuilders of Greenock, being launched on 6 June 1963 and commissioned on 16 September 1964. From 1973-76 she underwent an Ikara conversion at Devonport. The Ikara was an Australian designed missile that carried an ASW torpedo. In UK service the torpedo payload would be mounted onto the missile onboard resulting in the large structure forward of the bridge which housed the missile assembly room and the launcher. After decommissioning she was purchased by Devonport Management Limited with a view to selling her to an overseas customer, but this was not to be and in 1990, she was sold and broken up at Millom in Cumbria.

The first of the Type 23 frigates, HMS NORFOLK pictured arriving at Portsmouth on 16th November 1990. One of 16 ships, NORFOLK was built on the Clyde by Yarrow shipbuilders and completed in 1989. She was the first ship to be armed with the new Vertical Launch Sea Wolf missile system and was also fitted with 2 quadruple Harpoon missile launchers. She had her original 4.5-inch gun replaced with the more modern Mk 8 mod 1. NORFOLK decommissioned in 2005 and was sold to Chile together with her sisters MARLBOROUGH and GRAFTON. All three were refitted at Portsmouth by BAE Systems in a multi-million pound deal to prepare them for service with the Chilean Navy. In 2006 NORFOLK was commissioned as ALMIRANTE COCHRANE.

RNAL 54 aground near Southsea Castle was photographed on 30th January 1990. Classified as a Royal Naval Air Lighter, she and sister vessels were used to transport aircraft to and from shore side to aircraft carriers in harbour or at sea. Although self propelled she was, at the time, under tow and broke free in a gale and drifted ashore. She was refloated at the next high tide by tugs from Portsmouth naval base.

On a breezy morning in May 1992 HMS ARK ROYAL steams up the River Clyde on a courtesy visit to Glasgow. Completed in 1985 by Swan Hunter on the Tyne she was the third and last of the Invincible class aircraft carriers to be completed for the Senior Service. She was originally to have been named INDOMITABLE but this was changed due to the public reaction to the loss of the previous ARK ROYAL when she paid off in 1979. She saw service in the 90's during the Bosnian conflict and was also in action during the invasion of Iraq in 2003. She attended the Canadian Navy's Centennial Review at Halifax, Nova Scotia in the summer of 2010. ARK ROYAL paid off at Portsmouth on 11th March 2011, sooner than anticipated - a victim of further defence cuts. She was sold to Turkish ship breakers and left Portsmouth in tow on 20th May 2013.

MV NORTHELLA, a former Hull trawler photographed leaving Portsmouth on 16th March 1992. She was chartered to the MoD and used as a Navigation training ship. She was built at Wallsend by Clelands Ship Building Company and completed in 1973 for her owners J. Marr and Sons, Hull. At the start of the Falklands War in 1982 she and four other deep sea trawlers were taken over by the Royal Navy and commissioned for service and operated as minesweepers in the South Atlantic. All five returned to Rosyth later in that year and were returned to their owners. During her second period with the MoD she operated out of Portsmouth for several years under the red ensign. She went to Indian ship breakers in 2005.

RMAS SALMOOR, one of three large Sal class mooring and salvage vessels, all built by Hall Russell at Aberdeen. SALMOOR was completed in 1985. She is seen in May 1992 returning to her base at Great Harbour, Greenock. She was renamed SD SALMOOR on the disbandment of the Royal Maritime Auxiliary Service and taken over by the commercial company Serco Denholm. SD SALMOOR was at Portsmouth in 2011 and sold by Serco in 2012 to Hays Ships Ltd and was named KOMMANDOR IONA. She was converted in the private sector and now undertakes subsea surveying operations. All three Sal class have been disposed of.

HMS URSULA, one of four Type 2400 submarines, seen arriving at HMS DOLPHIN in June 1992. The name ship and first of the four Upholder class was built at Barrow, the remaining three being constructed by Cammell Laird at Birkenhead, URSULA completing in 1992. All four were initially based at Gosport but later transferred to Devonport. The UK government determined that there was no longer a requirement to operate a convential submarine class alongside its nuclear-powered examples and all were withdrawn from service by the end of 1994. It was intended to find a buyer for them so they were placed in reserve at Barrow-in-Furness. In 1998 all four were purchased for service with the Canadian Navy and in 2003 URSULA was commissioned as HMCS CORNER BROOK.

The Ton class MCMV HMS NURTON arriving at Portsmouth on 14th December 1993, flying a very long paying off pennant. She is escorted by the Queens Harbour Master, who is seen saluting the Commander-in-Chief. NURTON was the last operational Ton in service with the RN. Her final commission was with the Northern Ireland Squadron. She was built at Belfast by Harland and Wolff and was completed in 1957. She was allocated to Tay division RNR being renamed MONTROSE. Her original Mirrlees V12 engines were replaced by high speed Napier Deltics during a refit in Portsmouth Dockyard in the early 1960's. A later refit, also at Portsmouth, from September 1964 to December 1965 saw her emerge as a Minehunter with Type 193 sonar installed. She was sold for breaking up in 1995.

XSV EXPRESS paying off at Portsmouth on 13th March 1994 on the disbandment of the Royal Naval Auxiliary Service (RNXS). Built in 1988 by Vosper Thornycroft, EXPRESS was one of four P2000 patrol craft built specifically for use by the auxiliary service. The RNXS also operated Loyal class fleet tenders similar to the Criccieth type and several former Ham class inshore minesweepers. After paying off she recommissioned as HMS EXPRESS and joined other P2000s as tenders to the University Royal Naval units. In total 16 of the class were built. Some have served as guardships at Cyprus and Gibraltar with the local squadron and currently two operate as guardships at Faslane providing security during submarine movements. EXPRESS is attached to the University of Wales URNU.

The former River class minesweeper HMS ARUN at Portsmouth on 31st May 1994. When new she joined the 10th Minesweeping Squadron as tender to HMS SUSSEX RNR unit and was based at Shoreham. She was transferred for duties with the Northern Ireland Squadron in 1993, along with other ships of the River class. The photograph shows her passing HMS DOLPHIN. As was the norm with Northern Ireland units her pennant number was removed from her hull. Along with 6 others in her class she was sold for service with the Brazilian Navy and renamed BABITONGA.

The Coastal Survey Vessel HMS BEAGLE at Portsmouth on 26th September 1997. One of a class of four, all built at Lowestoft by Brooke Marine, and completed in 1968. BEAGLE and BULLDOG were based at Portsmouth; FOX and FAWN at Devonport. All saw service throughout the world on surveying and updating charts. The hull was originally painted white and she had a buff funnel and mast. Although having been allocated a pennant number this was only added in later years when her hull and funnel were painted grey. Paid off in 2002 she was sold for conversion to a luxury yacht. Renamed TITAN she boasted accommodation for 22 guests in 11 'light and well proportioned staterooms'. She was noted for sale in 2015 for 14 million euros!

Heading out of Plymouth 2nd February 1998 is the former River class minesweeper HMS ORWELL. She was completed in 1985 and allocated to Newcastle division of the RNR as tender to HMS CALLIOPE. On paying off from the 10th MSS she replaced the Ton class minehunter HMS WILTON as the Training Ship attached to Britannia Royal Naval College at Dartmouth - note the Britannia emblem on the funnel. ORWELL decommissioned and was sold in 2001 for service with the Guyanan Defence Force and renamed ESSEQUIBO.

The oceangoing survey ship HMS HERALD at Portsmouth on 3rd July 1998 accompanied by the admiralty pilot cutter. She was built at Robb Caledon's ship-building yard at Leith and was commissioned late in 1974. The only ship in her class though similar to the earlier Hecla class which comprised three ships. Originally built to operate a Wasp helicopter her flightdeck was modified in 1988 to accommodate the larger Lynx. Like other survey ships of the Hecla class she was sent to the Falkland Islands to act as a hospital and ambulance vessel during the war in the South Atlantic returning to Portsmouth on 21st July 1982. She also saw service during the Gulf War deployed as a headquarters ship for the MCMVs. Originally painted in the standard colours of the Hydrographic fleet with white hull and buff funnel and mast, this was changed to Navy grey in the 1990's and her original pennant number A138 added. This was altered to H138 at a later date. Decommissioned in 2001 and sold to Irish commercial owners, who renamed her SOMERVILLE, she continued in service surveying in the Irish Sea.

RFA SEA CENTURION was built in Italy at Viareggio and launched as the Ro-Ro MV STENA AUSONIA as part of an order of five ships placed by Stena line. She was chartered by the MoD when additional freight carrying capacity was required following the decision to form the Joint Rapid Reaction Force in 1996. Commissioned into the Royal Fleet Auxiliary on completion in 1998, she was photographed leaving the Port of Southampton on 31st March 1999. She operated out of Marchwood Military Port until 2002 when she was returned to her owners. She was renamed MONT VENTOUX and saw commercial service in the Mediterranean between Marseilles and North Africa. She then became the STENA FORWARDER in 2005. Renamed ARK FORWARDER in 2007 for service between Tilbury and Gothenburg in Sweden and in the autumn of 2015 was operating as the WILHELMSBORG in the Gulf of Mexico.

The Type 23 frigate HMS GRAFTON pictured at Trieste, Italy on 23rd April 1999. She had just relieved her sister SOMERSET for policing duties in the Adriatic at the time of the third Balkan war. Built by Yarrow on the Clyde she was completed in 1997. In 2003, the ship was used in the ITV drama series *Making Waves* as the fictional HMS SUFFOLK - the series failed to emulate the success of *Warship* in the 1970s and was withdrawn from the schedules after only a couple of episodes. In 2004 she saw service in the Persian Gulf. In July of that year it was announced that she was to be paid off and was duly decommissioned in 2006. Along with two others in the class, she was sold for service with the Chilean Navy. After refit at Portsmouth she was named ALMIRANTE LYNCH.

The preserved Town class light cruiser HMS BELFAST is towed from Portsmouth on 10th July 1999 after dry docking. Built by Harland and Wolff at their shipyard in the city after which she was named she was commissioned in 1939. Later in that year she was seriously damaged when she hit a mine. It wasn't until 1942 that she returned to service following extensive repairs. She saw action on convoy duties, and was part of the fleet supporting the allied landings at Normandy in 1944. She went on to the Far East prior to the end of the war in the Pacific. She again saw action, this time during the Korean War in the early 1950's. After further service BELFAST was paid off into reserve in 1963. In 1971 she was brought to London and moored on the south bank of the Thames up river from Tower Bridge and opened to the public. In June 1999 she was towed to Portsmouth where her hull was shot blasted and repainted, leaving under tow the following month to return to her berth in the Pool of London.

Photographed on 7th August 2002, in an incomplete state berthed alongside at La Seyne-Sur-Mer, near Toulon in the South of France. She was ordered by Stena Line Sweden from the Viareggio yard of Italian shipbuilders, Esercizio and laid down as the STENA HISPANIA but launched, in 1998, as SEA CHIEFTAIN. The intention was that, on completion, she would be chartered by the MoD and would join the Royal Fleet Auxiliary as a sister to RFA SEA CENTURION. Later in 1998 the shipyard ran into financial difficulties. At that time SEA CHIEFTAIN was about 50% complete but the MoD cancelled the contract and she never served with the RFA. She was towed from Italy to La Seyne, where she would remain for about six months, before being towed back to Italy where most of the work to complete her was carried out at the Arsenale Shipyard in Venice emerging as the STENA SEAFREIGHTER in 2004. Renamed STENA FREIGHTER and was initially employed by her original owners Stena on their Travemunde to Gothenburg service. As of October 2015 she was still in service operating between Cagliari in Sardinia and Vado Ligure, a port in North West Italy.

The former HMS STALKER seen alongside at Pounds ship breaking yard at Tipner, Portsmouth on 26th February 2003, partially dismantled. She was built at Esquimalt, Canada at the yard of Canadian Yarrow. She was one of a numerically large class of Landing Ship Tanks designated LST (3), some of which were built in the UK, but many constructed in Canada. Built as LST 3515 and completed in June 1945 she was renamed STALKER in 1947. She was reclassified as a submarine support ship in 1958 and operated in Northern Ireland. Latterly she was employed at Rosyth as a security vessel, berthed across the entrance to drydocks when nuclear-powered submarines were undergoing refit. She was sold in 2002, initially with the hope of being preserved, but discussions with heritage and preservation groups failed and demolition began in 2010.

HMS ENDURANCE seen at Spithead on 27th June 2005 on rehearsal day for the Trafalgar 200 Fleet Review, celebrating the RN victory at the Battle of Trafalgar in 1805. Built in Norway as the Icebreaker MV POLAR CIRCLE in 1990, she was chartered as a replacement for the earlier ENDURANCE by the MoD in 1991. She was initially commissioned as HMS POLAR CIRCLE and in 1992 was purchased outright by the MoD and given the name HMS ENDURANCE. In December 2008, whilst on an 18-month deployment to the Antarctic, she suffered serious flooding of her machinery spaces, resulting in the near loss of the ship. Towed to Punta Arenas in Chile, she was eventually returned to Portsmouth aboard the semi-submersible vessel MV TARGET in 2009. Since her return she has been laid up in No 3 Basin in Portsmouth Naval Base. It is anticipated that she will be sold for breaking up in 2016.

HMS CLYDE photographed on 3rd August 2008 shortly before deploying to the Falklands. She commissioned in 2007 and is seen on trials in the Solent. Built by the Vosper Thornycroft Group, she was the last ship to be completed for the Royal Navy in Portsmouth Dockyard. A modified River class patrol vessel, she differs from her three sisters by having 30 mm gun, as well as an aft deck strengthened for aircraft operations. She has replaced LEEDS CASTLE and DUMB-ARTON CASTLE in the role of Falkland Islands Patrol Ship, a task which used to be alternated between her predecessors. CLYDE has remained on station in the South Atlantic since arriving in 2008. With her crews rotating on a regular basis from the UK, she is not expected to return home until 2018.

RFA FORT ROSALIE is seen leaving Devonport Dockyard on 31st March 2009 assisted by three Adept class tugs operated by Serco. She was built as the RFA FORT GRANGE by Scott Lithgow on the Clyde completing in 1978. One of two Fort class stores ships, they have replenishment facilities for both ammunition and general naval and victualling stores. Both have extensive aviation facilities with a single spot flight deck and full size hangar. The roof of the hangar was also strengthened for use as an emergency landing spot which enables them to operate up to four Sea King helicopters. She served in both the Falklands War and the 1st Gulf War. From 1997-2000 she served at Split as an accommodation and storage ship for food and ammunition for the British Forces operating in Croatia. In 2000 she was renamed FORT ROSALIE to avoid confusion with the newly commissioned RFA FORT GEORGE.

The Ocean Survey Vessel HMS SCOTT, photographed from Devils Point at Plymouth, outbound from her base at Devonport dockyard on 13th July 2009. This was shortly before being sent to the Falkland Islands to cover for the damaged HMS ENDURANCE in her role as Ice Patrol Ship. She was again deployed to the South Atlantic in 2010. Built at Appledore Shipbuilders at Bideford and completed in 1997 as a replacement for the survey ship HMS HECLA which was disposed of in the same year. She can remain at sea for up to 300 days a year, thanks to her novel crew rotation system. Her complement of 78 is divided into three sections: two sections are required to keep the ship operational, with the third on shore on leave or in training.

Landing Platform Dock (LPD), HMS ALBION at Portsmouth on 24th July 2009. She is one of two sister ships, both built at Barrow by BAE Systems. ALBION was completed in 2003 and HMS BULWARK in the following year. They replaced the LPD FEARLESS and INTREPID in service. They have a dock, below the flight deck, accessed via a stern door. This can accommodate up to four large LCUs capable of moving a Challenger tank from ship to shore. They also carry four smaller LCVPs in davits, for landing personnel and light vehicles ashore. Troops and equipment can also be moved by helicopter from a large flight deck. The rather squat appearance of the superstructure is due to a deck level being deleted during build as a cost saving measure. Retention of this deck would have permitted the inclusion of a helicopter hangar, enabling aircraft to be embarked and maintained away from the elements. Both ships are based at Devonport. As an economy measure, only one remains operational, while the other is laid up. In 2015 ALBION began a regeneration refit to return her to service in place of BULWARK.

HMS INVINCIBLE was photographed leaving Portsmouth for the last time on 24th March 2011. Towed by the tug SIROCCO, she was destined for the breakers yard at Aliaga in Turkey. Her sister HMS ARK ROYAL followed her to the same ship dismantlers in May 2013. Note the increased ski-jump angle compared to her original configuration (*see page 28*). Note also the reshaped bow, with a raised bulwark and the anchors no longer recessed. By the end of their careers all three Invincible class ships had also lost their Sea Dart missile system, the area being plated over to provide greater parking area for aircraft - the forward flight-deck extension can be seen projecting from the starboard bow.

The nuclear powered submarine HMS ASTUTE photographed in Southampton water on 6th April 2011, at the start of a courtesy visit to the Port of Southampton. ASTUTE was escorted by Serco tugs, based at Portsmouth, to her berth in the docks. Built at Barrow-in-Furness she was completed in 2009 the first of a proposed class of seven to replace the earlier Trafalgar class nuclear submarines. At 7,400 tonnes the Astute class submarines are 50% larger than their predecessors. In late 2011, she began a 5-month deployment to the US Navy's Atlantic Undersea Test and Evaluation Centre in the Bahamas, during which she fired Spearfish torpedoes and Tomahawk missiles. Her first operational deployment took place in 2014, returning to Faslane in October after eight months away.

One of the Type 22 Batch 3 frigates, HMS CAMPBELTOWN outbound from Devonport on 5th July 2010. She was built by Cammell Laird at Birkenhead and was commissioned in 1989. The Batch 3 ships were the most heavily armed of the Type 22s, reintroducing the 4.5-inch gun and replacing the four MM38 Exocet missiles with eight Harpoon missiles. In 2004 she was attached to STANAVFORLANT, the NATO squadron. She also saw service in the Persian Gulf during 2007-8. Late in her career she emerged from refit with hull strengthening clearly visible above her pennant number. CAMPBELTOWN was paid off in 2011 at Plymouth. She was later moved to lay up at Portsmouth where she would remain until being towed away for breaking up in Turkey in 2013.

HMS MONTROSE steams through Plymouth Sound on 14th July 2011. She was laid down in November 1989 by Yarrow Shipbuilders on the Clyde, and was launched on 31 July 1992. She commissioned in June 1994 and has had a demanding career ever since. She has been deployed to the South Atlantic as Falklands Guard ship on more than one occasion and enjoyed several NATO deployments prior to her first refit which ended in 2004. Since then she returned to the Gulf in 2006, spent seven months of the following year in NATOs Mediterranean squadron before once more deploying to the Gulf in 2008. The cycle of deployments continued until she entered her second refit period in 2014, from which she was scheduled to rejoin the fleet in 2016. Her original Mk.8 4.5-inch gun has been replaced by the later all electric Mod 1 variant, distinguishable from its predecessor by the angular turret.

Portsmouth based tugs SD INDEPENDENT and SD BOUNTIFUL photographed from the Round Tower on 28th July 2011 providing an escort to the Type 23 frigates HMS IRON DUKE and HMS RICHMOND on return from their deployments. Both tugs are firing their water cannons, all part of the ceremonial entry into harbour. SD INDEPENDENT was built at Damen's Gorinchem yard in the Netherlands in 2009 and is one of two ASD 2509 tugs based at Portsmouth. SD BOUNTIFUL, another from the same builders but this time from their Stellendam shipyard, was completed in 2010. She is one of a class of four of the ATD 2909 type. She is operated by her owners Serco Marine Services whilst her three sisters are in service at the Faslane submarine base on the Clyde.

The Ice Patrol Ship HMS PROTECTOR leaves her base at Portsmouth on 29th August 2011. Originally an icebreaker built in 2001 and registered in Norway as the MV POLARBJORN, she was chartered by the MoD in 2011 as a temporary replacement for the damaged HMS ENDURANCE and commissioned as HMS PROTECTOR in June 2011. She was purchased outright for RN service in 2013. Unlike previous ice patrol ships, she does not have a hangar and therefore is unable to deploy with a helicopter. To overcome this deficiency she is equipped with a large range of boats, including a landing craft, which are capable of transporting stores and personnel from ship to shore. Her home port was changed to Devonport in 2014.

HMS DRAGON photographed at Portsmouth arriving from her builders BAE at Scotstoun on the Clyde on 31st August 2011. She was the fourth of six Type 45 Daring class to be completed and was commissioned in 2012. She is affiliated to Cardiff and has a red Welsh Dragon emblazoned on her bow. Initially it was thought that this was a temporary feature, but the dragon has reappeared on the bows at various times throughout the vessel's short career to date! The Type 45 is an air warfare destroyer, her capability being centred around the PAAMS (Sea Viper) air-defence system utilising the SAMPSON active electronically scanned array (AESA) multi-function radar and the S1850M long-range radar.

The Type 42 destroyer HMS LIVERPOOL photographed inbound at Portsmouth on 17th February 2012 after escorting a Russian naval task group through the English Channel. The last of the Batch 2 Type 42s in service, she was built by Cammell Laird at Birkenhead, just the other side of the River Mersey from the city from where she took her name, and completed in 1982. Her first commission took her to the South Atlantic where she saw service in the Falkland Islands though this was after hostilities had ended. Compare her cluttered deck layout to that of her sisters (*see page 104*) - after the 1982 conflict attention was given to close in protection and therefore her boats were landed and Phalanx CIWS added on sponsons either side of the funnel. In March 2011 she was involved with the NATO naval blockade of Libya. LIVER-POOL was decommissioned at Portsmouth on 30th March 2012 and after lay up she was towed to Turkey by the Tug PANTODYNAMOS on 22nd October 2014 to be broken up.

HMS TIRELESS in Southampton water, photographed on 6th March 2012. She had been on a courtesy visit to the city and was outbound to the east via the Nab Tower, escorted by two of the Portsmouth based Serco tugs. Built by Vickers at Barrow and completed in 1985, she was one of the Trafalgar class nuclear submarines. She suffered a serious problem with the cooling system for her reactor in 2000 and spent almost a year in Gibraltar rectifying the fault. Of note in this image are the array of sensors around the conning tower and the anechoic tiles covering the pressure hull. TIRELESS was paid off in 2014 and is currently laid up at Plymouth.

The survey vessel HMS ENTERPRISE heads into Portsmouth Naval Base on 4th May 2012. Together with her sister and name ship of the class HMS ECHO she was built by Appledore at their North Devon yard at Bideford, ENTERPRISE completing in 2003. The initial order for the two ships was placed with the Vosper Thornycroft group. However VT subcontracted the order for construction to the Devon Shipbuilders. Both vessels are based at Devonport and are classed as multi role hydrographic vessels. In 2015 ENTERPRISE was deployed in the Mediterranean tasked with countering the people smugglers and to rescue migrants crossing from North Africa to Europe.

Formerly operated by the Royal Maritime Auxiliary Service the fleet tenders SD MEON and SD MENAI are seen alongside at their Falmouth base. Both were built by Richard Dunston at their shipyard on the Humber and completed in the early 1980's. Both are operated as safety vessels in support of helicopters flying from RNAS CULDROSE. Photographed on the River Fal in July 2013 they are seen in the new Serco colour scheme where the old RMAS buff superstructure is now painted white.

HMS SCIMITAR leaves her berth at the old torpedo camber in the dockyard on 12th August 2013 for her daily patrol out into Gibraltar's Territorial Waters. Together with sister ship HMS SABRE they form the Royal Naval Gibraltar Squadron. Both vessels were built by Halmatic in 1988 for counter terrorism duties in Northern Ireland. SCIMITAR and SABRE were formerly HMS GREYFOX and HMS GREYWOLF respectively. Transferred for service in Gibraltar in 2002 to replace two P2000 patrol craft, TRUMPETER and RANGER which were returned to the UK.

The Type 45 destroyer HMS DARING pictured from North Head at the entrance to Sydney harbour on 4th October 2013. This was her first visit to Australia where she represented the Royal Navy at the Royal Australian Navy's International Review. Two days earlier she had anchored at Jervis Bay with other International naval units in preparation for entry into Sydney. DARING was the first of the Type 45 destroyers to be completed. She was built by BAE on the Clyde and commissioned on 23rd July 2009 at Portsmouth. In 2011 she was fitted with a pair of 'Phalanx Close-In Weapon Systems' mounted either side of her superstructure. Four of the class have now been fitted with two quad Harpoon launchers forward of the bridge, the equipment being taken from the decommissioned Type 22 Batch 3 frigates.

Index